Iniquity -

Sin - missing the mark?

But the fruit of the Spirit is love, joy,
peace, longsuffering, gentleness,
goodness, faith, meekness, temperance:
against such there is no law.

GALATIANS 5:22-23 (KJV)

Transgression - refers to presumptuous
It means to choose to intentionally to
disobey. willful tresspassing premeditated
continuing without repentance. Micah: 2:1

Inculcations - ~~sinking~~ instill knowledge by hoping it will sink in by repeating

Licentious - lacking in will power or
moral discipline, or being promiscuous

debauchery - crazy parties or wild nights
over indulging in some of lifes pleasures

LOVE

A MANY SPLENDORED THING

NATE HOLCOMB

Teliosi - perfect.

Prosagoge - leading or bringing into the presence of

Markrothumia - longsuffering

Epios - Gentleness, mild or kind

Agathos

Ou Arestos - good

Telios

Pistos faith

Pistis faithful.

Kardia - Heartily

aparneomi - deny

LOVE: A Many Splendored Thing

Printed in the United States of America

ISBN: 978-1-930918-36-8

Him Publishing
P.O. Box 960
Copperas Cove, TX 76522
www.HimPublishing.com

It's All About Him Publishing, Inc. is a ministry of
CHRISTIAN HOUSE OF PRAYER MINISTRIES, INC.
www.chop.org

TABLE OF CONTENTS

INTRODUCTION

How does one describe love? Love is interpreted many ways, depending on who we're asking. However, God is the author of love because He is love (1st Jhn 4:7-8). And, not only is God love, but God describes His love in John 3:16: "For God so loved the world that He gave His only Begotten Son…" Notice the phrase "God so loved." When we see "God so loved," "So" is indescribable. That's why I am sharing, "Love is a Many Splendored Thing."

When we consider the splendor of a thing, we speak of its brilliance, grandeur, glory or magnificence. In its original Latin root, the word carries the meaning of "*bright, shine, gleam or glisten.*"[1]

The love of God is a many splendored thing. His love is full of grandeur, glory, and magnificence; this is His nature. Like a kaleidoscope, God's love or the character of His love has many distinct qualities and expressions and these qualities have been revealed to us in Jesus the Son of the Living God.

In Matthew 16:16, Peter declared about Jesus, "*Thou art the Christ, the Son of the Living God.*" Jesus says to Peter, "*…Flesh and blood has not **revealed** this to you, but My Father who is in heaven* (vs.17 NKJV)." In other words, Jesus was saying to Peter, my Father in heaven has *unveiled* to you who I am.

Vine's Expository Dictionary of Old and New Testament Words translates the word revelation as *"apokalypsis." Apokalypsis* means to *"uncover or unveil, to take the cover off."*

When we speak of "the nature of a thing" in its Latin origin, it means the "constitution or essential qualities, principle of life."[2] Therefore, the revelation of God's love or its nature, it is the unveiling, the uncovering and disclosure of the very essence of God Himself; the very principle and foundation of life.

The American Heritage Dictionary states that revelation is *"God's disclosure of Himself."*

The writer of Hebrews further reveals the nature of God's love in chapter 1:3. The writer speaking of Jesus says, "Who being the ***brightness*** of His glory, and the "***express image***" of his person..." The word brightness in its original Greek form is translated as *"apaugasma."*[3] *Apaugasma* also carries the meaning of radiance, brilliance or effulgence.

The writer of Hebrews in essence declares that the Son (Jesus), being one with the Father, is in *Himself,* the magnificence, radiance, effulgence, brilliance and brightness of the Godhead's glory.

In the original Greek, the word "express" in Hebrews 1:3 is translated *"charakter"* and "image" is the word *"eikon."*[4] This phrase carries the meaning of manifestation and reproduction. Thus, Jesus Christ is the very impression, and the *exact reproduction of God's love* (character) nature.

This love is further expressed in the fruit of the Spirit which is the character of Christ: *"But the fruit of the Spirit is love, joy, peace, longsuffering, gentleness, goodness, faith, meekness, temperance: against such there is no law* (Gal. 5:22-23)."

Note in the text that the word *fruit* is singular, not plural. The Holy Spirit has only one fruit and that is love, which is God's nature. God's love is further seen and expressed in eight distinct traits:

Joy—love's strength
Peace—love's safety
Long-suffering—love's patience
Gentleness—love's conduct
Goodness—love's character
Faithfulness—love's loyalty
Meekness—love's humility
Temperance—love's victory

God packaged love in the person of His Son, Jesus. Everything Jesus said and did was love in action. In John 14:8, Phillip asked Jesus to "Show us the Father." Jesus replied, "He that hath seen me hath seen the Father." The same would be true if he had asked Jesus, "Show us love." Jesus could have responded, "He that hath seen me has seen love."

A popular saying in today's world is, "Show me some love." In other words, you have to show it, for others to know it. We want to begin with Jesus' very own words: "For I have given you an example, that ye should do as I have done to you (Jhn 13:15)." What Jesus has to say about love begins with His embryonic teaching of the Beatitudes and Sermon on the Mount.

The Beatitudes' teaching in essence is "Let this be you

peace, longsuffering, gentleness, goodness, faith, meekness, temperance: against such there is no law (Gal. 5:22-23)."

Note in the text that the word *fruit* is singular, not plural. The Holy Spirit has only one fruit and that is love, which is God's nature. God's love is further seen and expressed in eight distinct traits:

Joy—love's strength
Peace—love's safety
Long-suffering—love's patience
Gentleness—love's conduct
Goodness—love's character
Faithfulness—love's loyalty
Meekness—love's humility
Temperance—love's victory

God packaged love in the person of His Son, Jesus. Everything Jesus said and did was love in action. In John 14:8, Phillip asked Jesus to "Show us the Father." Jesus replied, "He that hath seen me hath seen the Father." The same would be true if he had asked Jesus, "Show us love." Jesus could have responded, "He that hath seen me has seen love."

A popular saying in today's world is, "Show me some love." In other words, you have to show it, for others to know it. We want to begin with Jesus' very own words: "For I have given you an example, that ye should do as I have done to you (Jhn 13:15)." What Jesus has to say about love begins with His embryonic teaching of the Beatitudes and Sermon on the Mount.

The Beatitudes' teaching in essence is "Let this be your

attitude." It's a reference to Christians' attitude and attributes, while the Sermon on the Mount deals with activities and actions.

In the book of Revelation, chapters two and three, Jesus confronts the seven churches. The first church is "Ephesus," and he addresses the problem of how this church left their first love (Rev. 2:4). The first love refers to God's kind of love, which is agape. Agape is the foundation for all manifestations.

The psalmist inquired: *"If the foundations be destroyed what can the righteous do* (Psa. 11:3)*?"* I know it uses the term, foundations; but the foundation to the foundations is God's kind of love.

In 1st Corinthians chapter twelve Paul taught, *"And yet shew I unto you a more excellent way (vs. 31)."* "Way" is the Greek word Hodus. It means road or path to travel. Agape-love is the "Way" and Love Is A Many Splendored Thing.

> *"Charity never faileth...And now abideth faith, hope, charity, these three; but the greatest of these is charity."* (1st Corinthians 13:8)

Acclaimed writer Oscar Hammerstein II wrote the following lyrics from the film *Out of My Dreams*: *"A bell is not a bell unless you ring it. A song is not a song unless you sing it. And love is not love unless it's given away."*[5] This quote sets a moral tone and a model for all to aspire.

The aim and goal of this book is to show the myriad facets of God's love through his Son Jesus Christ. It is also my desire that you the reader will develop in the love of God and distribute

His love to people you encounter. With God's love operating in us and through us may we become "*living epistles*" of God's love read of men and given away (2nd Cor. 3:3).

THE FRUIT OF THE SPIRIT
LOVE

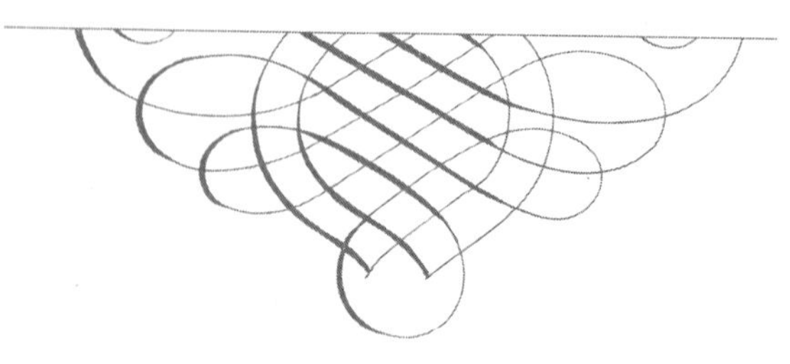

1

THE FOUR TYPES OF LOVE

*"But the fruit of the spirit is **love**..."*

(GALATIANS 5:22 BOLDNESS ADDED)

There are four types of love in the original Greek that are important for Christians to understand.

—Agape Love—

The first type of love is *Agape*. After His resurrection, Jesus appeared to His disciples. He asked Simon Peter: "*...Lovest thou me more than these...* (Jhn. 21:15)?" The word used here for *"Lovest thou me"* is agape. However, Peter answered: "*...Yea, Lord, thou knowest that I love thee...* (Jhn. 21:15)." Peter chose the phileo word love. Jesus asked the second time, "*...Lovest Thou me?"* Again, *"Agape thou Me?"* Peter answered Him with phileo. The third and final time Jesus recognized Peter's inability to comprehend and express agape-love, so He asked Peter on his level, "*... Lovest thou me* (phileo-love)*?*" Again, Peter's answer was the same. Phileo is good, but not the best. We need to express God's agape.

Picture this! There is nothing we have done to warrant God's unconditional love and there is nothing we can ever do to cancel it. Jesus is the Agape-love personified. Whatever He said and did was love expressing itself. He taught one of the most difficult aspects of loving God first:

> *"While he yet talked to the people, behold, his mother and his brethren stood without, desiring to speak with him. Then one said unto him, Behold, thy mother and thy brethren stand without, desiring to speak with thee. But he answered and said unto him that told him, Who is my mother? and who are my brethren? And he stretched forth his hand toward his disciples, and said, Behold my mother and my brethren! For whosoever shall do the will of my Father which is in heaven, the same is my brother, and sister, and mother."* (Matthew 12:46-50)

For some it's difficult not preferring family and friends above God. Here, Jesus models God must come first and final. Most people picture Jesus with a soft tone and touch, never dealing with hard issues. However difficult, Jesus expressed what I believe is tough love.

The following must become a philosophy that we adopt: *"I'm going with God and I don't care who it separates me from or identifies me with!"* Any philosophy less than this is idolatry. This is agape: loving God first—first love. Love is a Many Splendored Thing.

Agape love is the highest level of love possible—it's simply the ***Father's Love.***

—PHILEO LOVE—

In John 21, Peter responded to Jesus' question about love with the second type of love, "*phileo.*" This love is for those near and dear to our hearts. It is a brotherly love.

This is what William Penn, an English Quaker envisioned when he founded the city of Philadelphia in 1682, the "*City of Brotherly Love.*" The literal meaning of Philadelphia in the Greek language is a compound of two words, "*philos*" (loving), and "*adelphos*" (brother).[6]

Penn believed Philadelphia could be a place where anyone of any color or background could live together in peace and harmony from the perspective of "*loving your brother.*" Hebrews 13:1 says: "*Let brotherly love continue.*"

Phileo is affection, friendship and brotherly love. This refers to affections above emotions. Colossians 3:2 states: "Set your affection on things above, not on things on the earth."

One of the greatest revelations is learning how to love like God loves. Love is a many splendored thing. A scripture that will help us with this concept is: "*Learn to do well* (Isa. 1:17)." Whatever we do in life, if we don't' learn to do it, very likely we won't do it well. There of course is a danger in learning to do well. That is, we can become weary in what we are doing. The Scripture teaches: "*And let us not be weary in well doing* (Gal. 6:9)." I believe this is why our Lord Jesus asked Peter "Do you love me?"

Love for others motivates us, and overrides our being weary. Parents work because they love (phileo) their children and are willing to make sacrifices. Whatever assignment the Lord gives us, He wants us to do it because we love Him, as Father and as friend. That's agape and phileo.

When we learn to love, it will always be "well done." Love becomes our motivation and inspiration while we avoid becoming weary in well-doing.

Jesus became weary (Jhn. 4:6). Albeit, notice He was wearied in His journey, not in the work. The moment the woman of Samaria came to the well, Jesus revived and began ministering because He always did those things that pleased the Father (Jhn. 8:29).

Phileo is friendship love, called brotherly love. The Bible declares: *"A friend loveth at all times, and a brother is born for adversity* (Prov. 17:17)." To love with phileo is to love with affection. It's not based on conditions; that's storge (family love) or, eros (emotional love), which are predicated on feelings. The Scripture records: *"A man that hath friends must shew himself friendly: and there is a friend that sticketh closer than a brother* (Prov. 18:24)."

The intent of phileo, (brotherly love) is to love the brethren like friends, and friends like brothers. One of the first family problems was a conflict between two brothers, Cain and Abel.

> *"And Cain talked with Abel his brother: and it came to pass, when they were in the field, that Cain rose up against Abel his brother, and slew him. And the LORD said unto Cain, Where is Abel thy brother?* ***And he said, I know not: Am I my brother's keeper?"*** (Genesis 4:8-9 boldness added)

The answer to Cain's question was, "Yes!" If you are not your brother's keeper, you are your brother's killer. You are your brother's keeper through phileo-love. You have to love your brother like a friend.

> *"Let love be without dissimulation. Abhor that which is evil; cleave to that which is good. Be kindly affectioned one to another with brotherly love; in honour preferring one another."* (Romans 12:9-10)

As an example of phileo-love, Jesus taught a parable about a friend who went to His Friend, because a friend came to him in need. The parable portrays three friends (Lu. 11:5-8). There are two out of the three friends with small case 'f's.' Only one friend has a Capital 'F.' The two small case 'f's' represent us and Jesus. The capital 'F' represents God the Father. Remember, Hebrews 2:11 declares: *"For both he that sanctifieth and they who are sanctified are all of one: for which cause he is not ashamed to call them brethren..."* We are Jesus' brethren, and He loves us like His friends.

Phileo is ***Friendship Love.***

—Storge Love—

The third type of love is ***"storge."*** Romans 12:10 provides us with the only citation of this type of love recorded in the Bible. *Storge* has its origin in the compound word *"phileostorgos."*[7] *Phileo* (loving) and *storgos* (family love). *Storge* is the bond among mothers, fathers, sisters and brothers.

The Bible declares:

"Love one another with brotherly affection [as members of one family], giving precedence and showing honor to one another." (Romans 12:10 AMP)

Paul admonished the church at Rome to love one another with both "*phileo" (brotherly)* and "*storge*" (*family*) love.

There are many examples of family love found in Scripture, such as the love and mutual protection among Noah and his wife, their sons and daughters-in-law (Gen. 6:18). We also see the love that Jacob had for Rachael (Gen. 29:11-30); and the strong love the sisters Martha and Mary had for their brother Lazarus (Jhn. 11:30-44).[8]

The family in ancient Jewish culture was the bedrock of the community. In the 10 Commandments, God charges His people:

"Honor thy father and thy mother: that thy days may be long upon the land which the LORD thy God giveth thee." (Exodus 20:12)

The Apostle Paul commands:

"Children, obey your parents in the Lord: for this is right. Honor thy father and mother; (which is the first commandment with promise;) That it may be well with thee, and thou mayest live long on the earth." (Ephesians 6:1-3)

Storge is love for natural family but it is also to be expressed within our spiritual or church family. We are a family of children that have been adopted by God as His sons and daughters

(2 Cor. 6:17-18; Rom. 8:16-17). The Christian is to live as a family member with his brothers and sisters; he is to live being both kind and affectionate (Rom. 12:10). There is no dissension or divisiveness in love. The church is to live in love, and living in love is peace. *Storge is **Family Love.***

—Eros Love—

The fourth and final type of love is ***"eros."*** Although this Greek term does not appear in the Bible, "*eros*", or erotic love, is metaphorically seen in the Old Testament book, *The Song of Solomon.*[9] *Eros* is what we feel or that which is aroused in us toward our spouse. It can be stated as ***Feeling Love.***

> *"Let him kiss me with the kisses of his mouth! [She cries. Then, realizing that Solomon has arrived and has heard her speech, she turns to him and adds] For your love is better than wine!"* (Song of Solomon 1:2 AMP)

> *"Behold, you are beautiful, my love! Behold, you are beautiful! You have doves' eyes. [She cried] Behold, you are beautiful, my beloved [shepherd], yes, delightful..."* (Song of Solomon 1:15-16 AMP)

In the *Mishnah*, Rabbi Akiba (A.D. 50–135), the founder of rabbinic Judaism, said: "In the entire world there is nothing equal to the day on which the Song of Solomon was given to Israel. All the writings are holy, but the Song of Songs is most holy."[10] God is not opposed to being intimate with His people.

Eros is the love that is intended and limited to a husband and wife. God created human beings, male and female (Gen. 1:26-28) and instituted marriage in the Garden of Eden (Gen. 2:18, 21-24). Within the boundaries of marriage, it is "*eros*" love that is the physical, sensual love intended both for pleasure between a husband and wife and an emotional and spiritual bonding for the purpose of procreation as God designed it.

The Apostle Paul noted:

> "*Now to the unmarried and the widows I say: It is good for them to stay unmarried, as I do. But if they cannot control themselves, they should marry, for it is better to marry than to burn with passion.*" (1st Corinthians 7:8-9 NIV)

The Father's Love is the only unconditional love. The Apostle John knew the Father's love and thus wrote:

> "*Hereby perceive we the **love of God,** because he laid down his life for us: and we ought to lay down our lives for the brethren. But whoso hath this world's good, and seeth his brother have need, and shutteth up his bowels of compassion from him, how dwelleth the **love of God** in him? My little children, let us not **love** in word, neither in tongue; but in deed and in truth. And this is his commandment, That we should believe on the name of his Son Jesus Christ, and **love one another,** as he gave us commandment.*" (1st John 3:16-18, 23 boldness added)

"For God so loved the world, that he gave his only begotten Son, that whosoever believeth in him should not perish, but have everlasting life." (John 3:16)

The four types of love discussed in this chapter are important for Christians to understand. They express in various ways love is a many splendored thing.

I need to be married or Ima burn in Hell

My Hot Chocolate Muscle Man of God Please respond to the leadings and prompting of God concerning me. He did put us together, be obedient, stop playing.

~~1. Agape 2. Storge 3~~

1. Agape (3)
2. Storge
3. Phileo (2)
4. Eros

1. Agape
2. Phileo
3. Storge
4. Eros

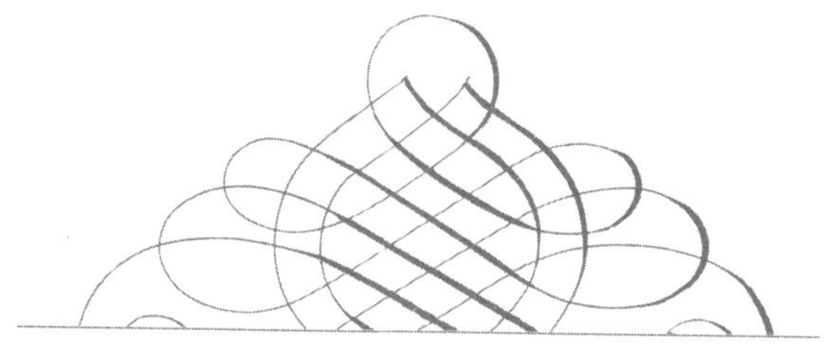

THE FRUIT OF THE SPIRIT
LOVE

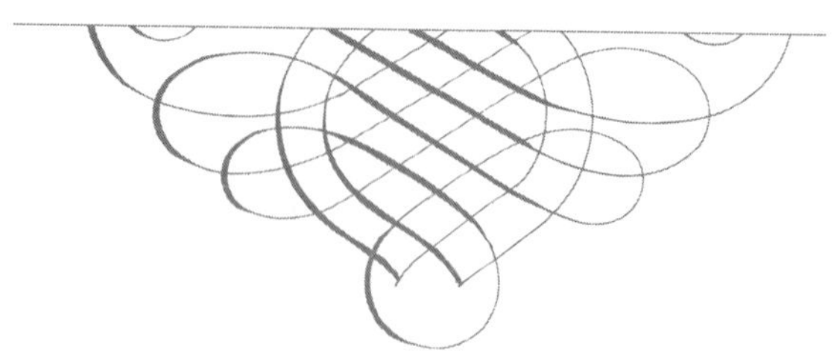

KEYS TO PERFECTED LOVE

"But the fruit of the spirit is ***love...****"*
(GALATIANS 5:22 BOLDNESS ADDED)

The following scripture states, if we love one another, God dwells in us. We not only *represent* God, we also want to *re-present* Him. Love is a many splendored thing and the only way we can re-present the Father is with a loving heart. God wants to dwell in us causing other people to sense and see His love on display through us.

> *"No man hath seen God at any time. If we love one another, God dwelleth in us, and his love is perfected in us."* (1st John 4:12)

—Love Like God Loves—

1st John 4:12(b) says: *"His love is perfected in us."* One of the most exciting things we can experience in our lives is to love as God loves. Vine's Expository Dictionary of Old and New

Testament Words translate the word "perfected" in this passage as the Greek word "*teleios.*" Teleios carries the meaning of "full-grown, complete, finished and mature."

When God dwells within us, we love one another and God's love becomes perfected, that is, complete and fulfilled in and through us. We can love like God loves. With God's love perfected in us we can even love our enemies.

So we're not left befuddled, Jesus tells us the way to love our enemies:

> "*...Bless them that curse you, do good to them that hate you, and pray for them which despitefully use you, and persecute you.*" (Matthew 5:44)

The keys for loving our enemies involve 3 edicts from the Lord:

1. Bless them
2. Do good to them
3. Pray for them

For a greater appreciation of these keys let's expound on the words bless, good and pray.

The word "bless" in the original Greek means "*to speak well of, to celebrate with praises.*"[11] God blesses us and then He uses us to be a blessing! Our English word "good" is the Greek word "*agathos.*" *Agathos* describes an act or action *that is good in its character or constitution and beneficial in its effect.*[12] The final aspect of the pattern is to pray (*proseuchomai)* for them.[13] *Proseuchomai* carries the connotation of *praying to God fervently; to pour one's whole heart and total being out to God.*

Solomon said:

> *"If thine enemy be hungry give him bread to eat; and if he be thirsty, give him water to drink: for thou shalt heap coals of fire upon his head, and the* LORD *shall reward thee."* (Proverbs 25:21-22)

The Apostle Paul speaking the same thing and having the same earnest care as Solomon concerning his enemies, declares to the church at Rome:

> *"Therefore if thine enemy hunger, feed him; if he thirst, give him drink: for in so doing thou shalt heap coals of fire on his head."* (Romans 12:20)

There are three types of people who are incapable of loving like God loves:

» **The Unsaved**—they will never love like God because they must be born from above in order to love like God.

» **The Unforgiving**—these people cannot love like God because their hearts are hardened.

» **The Unaware**—they are unaware they can love like God. Therefore, they are unaware of how to love people they don't like.

The Father's love is being perfected in us when we bless them that curse us, do good to them that hate us and pray for them that despitefully use and persecute us. Believe me; it is possible to love everyone.

Here is another key to perfected love, "*If you do something against someone that you dislike, you dislike the person more, but if you do something good to someone you dislike, you will dislike them less and even begin to like them!*"

Begin loving everybody and declare now, "I'm going to love like God loves!"

—THE COMMAND TO LOVE—

If we obey the command of the Lord to love our enemies, we begin liking people we never could have imagined.

The word "like" simply means *agreeable or have a friendly feeling towards someone or something.*[14] Perfected love has nothing to do with how we feel. It is a matter of our will.

Oftentimes, churches are not full because we lack in the perfected love of God. The love is in us; it's just not *perfected.* It is not full-grown, complete, finished or mature in us.

Colossians 3:14 reminds us: "*And above all these things put on charity (love), which is the bond of perfectness.*" The word bond in this text means a "*joint or ligament.*" Literally it means, "*Uniting principle.*"[15] This same scripture is written in the Message Bible: "*And regardless of what else you put on, wear love. It's your basic, all-purpose garment. Never be without it.*"

Consider the following passage:

> "*But when the Pharisees had heard that he had put the*

> *Sadducees to silence, they were gathered together. Then one of them, which was a lawyer, asked him a question, tempting him, and saying, Master, which is the great commandment in the law?*" (Matthew 22:34-36)

Jesus responded to the lawyer's question with the Shema of Israel. The Shema is the most important prayer in Judaism. It refers to Deuteronomy 6:4-5, which begins with the command to "*hear.*"

Jesus taught:

> "*...Thou shalt love the Lord thy God with all thy heart, and with all thy soul, and with all thy mind. This is the first and great commandment. And the second is like unto it, Thou shalt love thy neighbor as thyself. On these two commandments hang all the law and the prophets.*" (Matthew 22:37-40)

The bond, the joint or ligament that unites humanity is God's love. As believing Believers, the key to perfected love is to hear and obey the Lord. In our obedience to His commands, we are empowered and enabled to *bless, do good* and to even *pray* for our enemies to the Glory of God (Matt. 5:44). I trust the keys to perfected love will be recognized because love is a many splendored thing.

> "*...If we love one another, God dwelleth in us, and his love is perfected in us.*" (1st John 4:12)

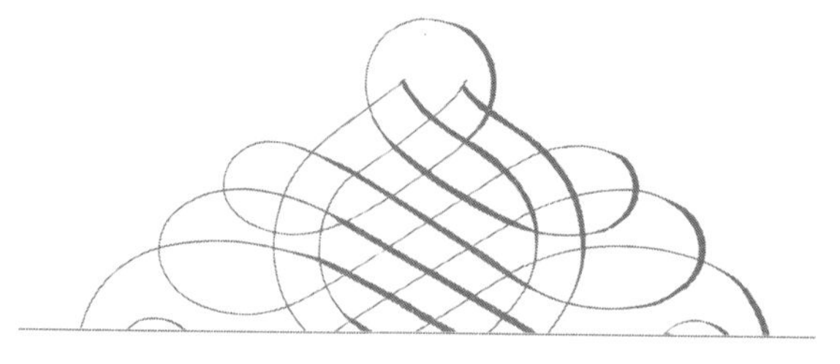

THE FRUIT OF THE SPIRIT
LOVE

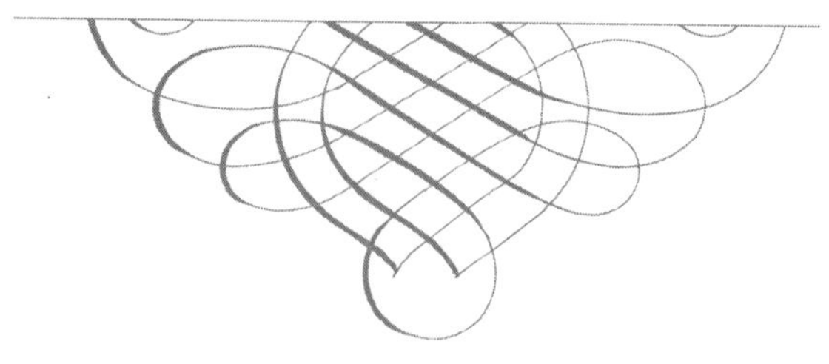

3

STAYING IN THE LOVE OF GOD

"But the fruit of the spirit is ***love...****"*

(GALATIANS 5:22 BOLDNESS ADDED)

When Jesus taught the people, He taught them how to love their enemies; and to love their neighbors as they loved themselves (Lu. 10:27). The Pharisees taught love your neighbor and hate your enemies (Matt. 5:43). That concept was contrary to Jesus' teaching and God's heart.

The following scripture admonishes us to keep ourselves in the love of God. The plot, ploy and plans of Satan are to get us out of God's love.

> *"Keep yourselves in the love of God, looking for the mercy of our Lord Jesus Christ unto eternal life. And of some have compassion, making a difference."* (Jude 21-22)

—LOVE IS THE FOUNDATION—

Jesus commented: *"Ye have heard that it hath been said, Thou shalt love thy neighbor, and hate thine enemy. But I say unto you, Love your enemies...* (Matt. 5:43-44)." God says, *"Husbands, love your wives...* (Eph. 5:25)." He tells parents to nurture their children, and children to obey their parents (Eph. 6:4; Col. 3:20).

Why did the Lord bother teaching this? He was teaching and telling us the foundation of all things is the love of God. Also, love is the foundation for all manifestations of God.

If we know how to love our enemies then we will know how to love everybody else. Everyday repeat this, *"I love God, myself, and everybody else!"* God's love is broad enough to reach everyone, the breadth and depth of it was the giving of His Son. Love is a many splendored thing!

As a foundation, God's love has drawing power. There is a magnetism that is connected to His love. The Bible says that we were drawn to God because of His goodness (Rom. 2:4). He commended His love to us while we were yet sinners (Rom. 5:8). We did not find God, God found us. Like moths to a flame, He called—we came.

God's love begins as a foundation, but must move to a manifestation. In other words, His love should change us from the inside out. The extent of our love is narrow and shallow. Usually, we only love them that love us, only greet them that greet us; and only give to them that give to us. However, God does not want that for His church. We can love as God loves.

—Stop In the Name of Love—

There was a professor who taught at seminary for over fifty years and then retired. He was known for teaching love. Whatever he taught, it always involved love. Whatever he preached, involved love.

He was known as "The Professor of Love." One day after his retirement, he was working on his driveway. Just as he finished pouring cement, children in the neighborhood ran across it with their dog, leaving foot prints behind.

He got so upset he ran into his garage, came out with a hoe and began swinging at the children and the dog!

His wife stepped out of the house and said, "For fifty years you've been teaching love. The whole neighborhood knows that you're about love. What's wrong with you? What are you doing?" He said, "Honey, I taught love in the abstract. This is love in the concrete." The point is we can talk about love. It sounds good, but we need to bring it in the concrete.

Ponder Jude 21 from three translations:

» "*Stay always within the boundaries where God's love can reach and bless you…*" (TLB)

» "*Staying right at the center of God's love…*" (MSG)

» "*Keep yourselves in the love of God…*" (KJV)

In an illustration, I had my wife Pastor Valerie stand in the center of a circle comprised of nine members of our church. The nine members represented the fruit of the Spirit as they surrounded her.

The important thing to consider was that the fruit of the Spirit (nine members) did not hold Valerie in place. It was her responsibility to stay within the fruit of the Spirit. The point is, when we keep ourselves in the love of God Satan cannot touch us.

In order for him to get to us he has to break through the love of God. If he successfully provokes us to step out of God's circle of love, he can inflict his will upon us. Thus, his goal is to bring us out. Just as it was Valerie's responsibility to stay within the fruit of the Spirit, it is incumbent upon us to do the same.

Remember, the plot, ploy, and plan of Satan is to get us out of the love of God. How do we stay in the love of God? The concept is simple, but can prove difficult. We must stop in the name of love! In essence, before we *act* we must *ask*, "Will this action bring glory or shame to God's name?"

The Bible says for us to learn to do well (Isa. 1:17). We must learn to *respond* and not *react*. In other words, we should never allow the panic buttons of life to push us out of the character of Christ.

How do we stay in the love of God? We stop in the name of love. Don't let the devil bring us out of God's love. Learn how to respond and not react.

John the Baptist said the following:

"He must increase, but I must decrease." (John 3:30)

Beloved, everything in the Bible is a revelation of a difference. And the revelation is what makes the difference. The following idea should not be reduced to mere semantics, it's a revelation. When the scripture says He must increase and we must decrease, that's what it means. It does not convey that we decrease first and then He increases in our lives. Quite the contrary, He must increase before we decrease. When Jesus increases, His love increases. The only right response to receiving God's love is to allocate it to others.

If the devil can get us to decrease first, then we succumb to depression or at least self-denial and there is no guarantee of Jesus' increased presence. Thus, we become drained of Christ's life and love. The way we decrease is by allowing the fruit of Jesus' Spirit to increase in our lives, first.

Again, staying in the love of God is accomplished by stopping in the name of love so He (Jesus) can increase and we will naturally decrease. If we do this, Jesus' character will be seen through the manifestation of the fruit of the Spirit. Jesus is on the inside of us working to get on the outside in order to make a change in our lives. If I stay in, He will come out!

A Sunday school teacher asked the class, "How do we resist the devil?" One little girl raised her hand and said, "I've learned that whenever the devil comes knocking on my door to let Jesus answer." This is what I'm talking about. We shouldn't answer; we shouldn't react, instead, we must respond by stopping in the name of love, and allowing Jesus to come out. Love is a many splendored thing!

> "*Ye are of God, little children, and have overcome them: because greater is he that is in you, than he that is in the world.*" (1st John 4:4)

When the devil comes to mess with our lives, we must let Jesus come out. We have to stay in God's neighborhood; the God zone. What is the God zone? It's God's life, light, and love. Stay in the life of God. Stay in the light of God. Stay in the love of God. *Stop in the name of God's love!*

—LOVE BUILDS CHARACTER—

God wants to build character in our lives. What kind of character does He want to build? He's looking to develop the character of Jesus through the love of God. God is cultivating within us the character of Jesus to defeat the enemy no matter how he approaches.

The Bible records:

> "*The LORD shall cause thine enemies that rise up against thee to be smitten before thy face: they shall come out against thee one way, and flee before thee seven ways.*" (Deuteronomy 28:7)

We are not to run from the enemy; the enemy will flee before us! My friend and brother in Christ, Evangelist Mickey Bonner was noted for saying, "When we know who we are *in Christ*, we can attack hell with an empty water pistol and the fire will be out before we get there!" We need to know who we are. God has armed us with His love, and "*love never fails* (1st Cor. 13:8)."

The following passage of scripture records the events which provoked Jesus to describe the Good Samaritan. This account is representative of the Father's unfailing love.

> *"And, behold, a certain lawyer stood up, and tempted him, saying, Master, what shall I do to inherit eternal life? He said unto him, What is written in the law? how readest thou? And he answering said, Thou shalt love the Lord thy God with all thy heart, and with all thy soul, and with all thy strength, and with all thy mind; and thy neighbor as thyself. And he said unto him, Thou hast answered right: this do, and thou shalt live. But he, willing to justify himself, said unto Jesus, And who is my neighbor?"* (Luke 10:25-29)

It is at this juncture of their conversation that Jesus began teaching about the Good Samaritan. A certain man traveled from Jerusalem (a heavenly state) and came into Jericho where he was roughed up by thieves.

A priest passed by this wounded Jew but had no compassion. Then there was a Levite (a church leader). Today he would be considered a pastor, deacon or an elder. He stopped long enough to look at the wounded man, but offered no assistance. Finally, there was a Samaritan (a despised rival), who exemplified compassion, and ministered to the fallen man's needs. The Good Samaritan typified the character of Christ.

God's love is compassion in action. His character is displayed through love, peace, and blessing. Many people may say I love you, but fail to *show it* allowing others to *know it.* People will not know love unless we show love.

To say we love and there is no compassion in action is counterfeit love. Love is not love unless we give it away; unless we can show it.

THE FRUIT OF THE SPIRIT

LOVE

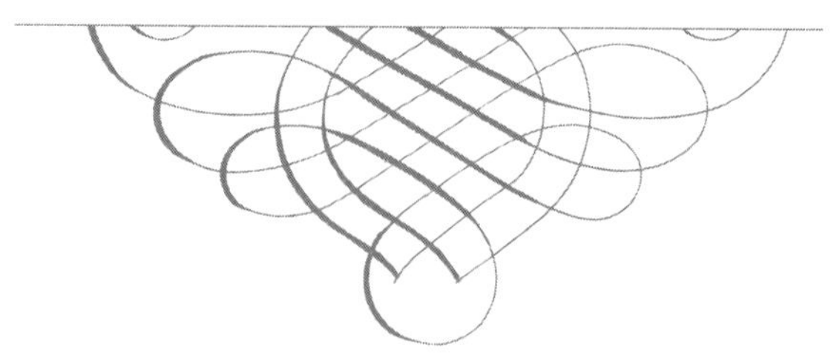

LOVING THOSE YOU DON'T LIKE

"But the fruit of the spirit is ***love****..."*

(GALATIANS 5:22 BOLDNESS ADDED)

In the passage below, Jesus communicated something profound about God's love; He commanded us to love our enemies. His statement, *"You have heard it has been said. . ."* was provoked by the Pharisees. These religious leaders twisted the Scripture by adding the phrase, *"Hate your enemy."*

However, Leviticus 19:18 records, "*Love thy neighbor as thyself.*" The verse does not say anything about hating your enemy. Thus, Jesus countered this false doctrine with, "*But I say unto you...*" In essence, Jesus gives us a stern admonishment to *love our neighbors* (Lev. 19:18) and *our enemies* (Matt. 5:44).

> "*Ye have heard that it hath been said, Thou shalt love thy neighbor, and hate thine enemy. But I say unto you, Love your enemies, bless them that curse you, do good to them that hate you, and pray for them which despitefully use you, and persecute you.*" (Matthew 5:43-44)

Love is a many splendored thing and through God's love we can do the uncomfortable and seemingly impossible—loving our enemies. There should be no doubt that loving our enemies is God's will. For many, the struggle is not with the will; it's with the way. The way to love others is by faith, through forgiveness, and beyond feelings. We must have faith in the Father's love; His love opens the path for forgiveness and is not motivated by feelings.

—LOVE BY FAITH—

"This is my commandment, that ye love one another, as I have loved you." (John 15:12)

Love is the essence of God's being. Loving those that you don't like is a matter of faith.

"And Jesus answering saith unto them, Have faith in God. For verily I say unto you, That whosoever shall say unto this mountain, Be thou removed, and be thou cast into the sea; and shall not doubt in his heart, but shall believe that those things which he saith shall come to pass; he shall have whatsoever he saith. Therefore I say unto you, What things soever ye desire, when ye pray, believe that ye receive them, and ye shall have them. And when ye stand praying, forgive, if ye have ought against any: that your Father also which is in heaven may forgive you your trespasses." (Mark 11:22-25)

Would you agree that an enemy could be considered a mountain? In other words, an enemy could be an obstruction or distraction. Even still, we must not allow enemies to hinder our progress in life. In order to maintain focus we must have faith in God. Through faith we love.

Jesus explicitly gave us a commandment to love our enemies. We must come to terms; He did not make a suggestion, He gave us a commandment. Therefore, it behooves us to follow this command.

We must believe God will protect us from evil people and vindicate us from evil speaking and accusations. Faith allows us to love without restrictions.

True faith works by love:

> *"For in Jesus Christ neither circumcision availeth any thing, nor uncircumcision; but faith which worketh by love."* (Galatians 5:6)

As an example, I offer one of my favorite stories:

A father was placing his porch furniture in the basement of his home. His little son was on the porch watching. The father lowered the furniture, then jump down into the basement to put it away. All of a sudden, a blackout hit the neighborhood.

Of course, the little boy was afraid and began to cry. His dad encouraged him not to be afraid because he was there. But, the boy cried, "I can't see you down in the basement." The father was able to see him because of a full moon. He said to his son, "You know I love you and won't drop you, son. Jump and I will catch you."

The son said, "But daddy, I can't see you." The father responded, "That's okay. I can see you; jump." By faith the son jumped, because "faith works by love."

In Mark the 11th chapter we are presented with the process of faith. First, we're given **the Person of our faith** (Mk. 11:22). Jesus did not simply say, have faith, but have "*faith in God.*" Faith has to have an object. And God, for a lack of better terms, is to be the object of our faith. Faith has no value in itself; only the object (God) has value.

Second, **the principle of our faith** is revealed (Mk. 11:23). The principle of our faith connotes that we have whatsoever we say. We can "say to the mountain," only after we've heard from God. Therefore, when we speak it's by faith and in love.

How does faith come? Faith comes by hearing the word of God. Then we can say what God tells us to say to any mountain, and the problem is removed. In this case, we say, "We love our enemies; we'll do good and pray for those who don't like us." This confession will yield great results.

The third point of emphasis is **the prayer of faith** (Mk. 11:24). Prayer without faith is neutered prayer. Prayer with faith is powerful. The prayer of faith mixed with love is powerful and productive. This power produces intimacy through prayer. We become intimate with the One we pray to (God). We become intimate with the ones we pray with (other Believers). We become intimate with the ones we pray for (in this case our enemies).

As we pray for our enemies with a sincere heart the strangest thing will occur. We'll become moved with compassion for them and eventually love will take the place of hate. Many people place a period after the prayer of faith, but that is not the end of the process.

The next principle is the final part—forgiveness. Many are reluctant to pardon their enemies. Due to this fact, their lives are marred with un-forgiveness. This unfortunate state is **the problem of faith** (Mk. 11:25). None of the promises Jesus gave will come to fruition, if we do not confront the problem of our faith.

—Love through Forgiveness—

"But if ye forgive not men their trespasses, neither will your Father forgive your trespasses." (Matthew 6:15)

As we tackle the question, "How do we love people we don't like?" It stands to reason, if a person is an enemy, they don't like us and usually the feeling is mutual. Nevertheless, this endeavor is possible if we do not confuse liking with loving. To like someone derives from how we feel. Alternatively, loving someone is an act of our will.

Jesus tells us to love (not like) our enemies. To accomplish this goal we must put aside our feelings and command our will to comply with God's. In order to avoid the problem of faith we must stand ready to forgive. Through forgiveness we keep other's offenses from becoming our stumbling blocks.

"Then said he unto the disciples, It is impossible but that ***offences*** *will come: but woe unto him, through whom they come! It were better for him that a millstone were hanged about his neck, and he cast into the sea, than that he should offend one of these little ones."* (Luke 17:1-2 boldness added)

We just read where Jesus said, *"It is impossible but that offenses will come."* The word offense is the Greek word *"scandalizo"* where we get our English word scandalize.[16]

Scandalize means *anything* that can give someone an occasion or *opportunity* to stumble or fall. It is when someone does something to someone that causes them to distrust and disbelieve something they would normally trust or believe.

Let's be honest, we have all scandalized someone at some point. Many would like to feel they've only been offended. However, the coin does have two sides. Yes, we have been offended, but we have been the offenders also.

Even in the face of major offenses we must maintain the capacity of forgiveness. One man who positively affected history and changed the course of the nation of South Africa through major acts of forgiveness was Nelson Mandela.

Mandela was sentenced to a life of imprisonment for his role in South Africa's struggle for racial equality. Before being sentenced, he delivered what became known as his, "Speech from the Dock:"

> *"I have fought against white domination, and I have fought against black domination. I have cherished the ideal of a democratic and free society in which all persons live together in harmony and with equal opportunities. It is an ideal which I hope to live for and to achieve. But if needs be, it is an ideal for which I am prepared to die."*

Throughout his imprisonment he rejected at least three offers of conditional release. This profound patriarch of South Africa refused comfort at the expense of compromise, and was eventually released on February 11, 1990.

After having spent almost three decades behind prison walls one would think Nelson Mandela's heart would have hardened. However, his actions displayed quite the opposite. Soon after his release, Mandela further immersed himself into the campaign for racial and ethnic equality.

Nelson Mandela received the Noble Peace Prize in 1993 and on May 10, 1994 was inaugurated South Africa's first democratically elected president. How could a man rise from prisoner to president? When we love through forgiveness, all things are possible. Mandela didn't allow his hard life to harden his heart.

Despite living through horrific conditions and the provocations of the adversary, his life served as an inspiration to all. His life taught us not to meet racism with rage, or deprivation with indignity; instead, we can love through forgiveness. Forgiveness helps erase scars caused by ignorance and indifference.

> *"What counts in life is not the mere fact that we have lived. It is what difference we have made to the lives of others that will determine the significance of the life we lead."*[17] —Nelson Mandela

The plan of the enemy is for us to allow the offenses of life to cause our hearts to become hardened. A hard heart lacks love and prohibits us from affecting our world. God will positively affect our world only through a believing heart not a bleeding heart.

Forgiveness allows our hearts to convert from those that bleed to those that believe.

It is possible for us to depart from the living God, if our hearts are not where God said they should be.

God says:

> *"This people draweth nigh unto me with their mouth, and honoreth me with their lips; but their heart is far from me."* (Matthew 15:8)

Jesus said, "*Take heed to yourselves* (Lu. 17:3)." The writer of Hebrews noted, "*Take heed, brethren lest there be in any of you an evil heart of unbelief, in departing from the living God (Heb. 3:12).*" In order to move into another dimension with God, we must allow Him to change our hearts. God can only change our hearts when we're willing to forgive those who have offended us.

Jesus taught this same message to His disciples:

> *"And if he trespass against thee seven times in a day, and seven times in a day turn again to thee, saying, I repent; thou shalt forgive him."* (Luke 17:4)

Peter came back and asked the Lord:

> *"...Lord, how oft shall my brother sin against me, and I forgive him? till seven times? Jesus saith unto him, I say not unto thee, Until seven times: but, Until seventy times seven."* (Matthew 18:21-22)

In this instance, Jesus was teaching the law of reciprocity.

Reciprocity is simply an exchange. If we forgive, it means we receive forgiveness. If we do not forgive, we create a roadblock. Many times God has answered our prayers, but they have been hindered because there is a roadblock of un-forgiveness.

The Bible records:

> *"Likewise, ye husbands, dwell with them according to knowledge, giving honour unto the wife, as unto the weaker vessel, and as being heirs together of the grace of life; that your prayers be not hindered."* (1st Peter 3:7)

Wow! Our prayers can be hindered based on a broken relationship with our spouse. How we treat one another can produce a roadblock, a hindrance to our prayers.

Picture this! You have ordered some furniture and have been waiting all morning for the delivery. Finally, the delivery man calls and tells you that he has your furniture, but there is a roadblock hindering him from getting to your house. He further explains as soon as the roadblock is removed he will deliver your furniture.

For some of us, it's not that our prayers have not been heard, God is unable to deliver answers due to the roadblock. The hindrance of un-forgiveness needs to be removed.

Forgiveness is a powerful tool in loving those that you don't like but a lot of people refuse to use it. Some people can go days, months and years without having said, "Forgive me" to anyone.

The message in the following passage is forgive me as I forgive others:

"After this manner therefore pray ye: Our Father which art in heaven, Hallowed be thy name. Thy kingdom come. Thy will be done in earth, as it is in heaven. Give us this day our daily bread. And forgive us our debts, as we forgive our debtors." (Matthew 6: 9-12)

LOVE BEYOND FEELINGS

Many of us want to *represent* Christ, that's good, but it's not enough. Christ wants us to *re-present* Him! To represent Christ means He is not there. However, to *re*-present Christ is to let Christ *come out* and who we are stay in. Love is a many splendored thing. This is why the Lord compels us to love. Only with Christ residing in us are we able to achieve great things and love in great measure.

"To whom God would make known what is the riches of the glory of this mystery among the Gentiles; which is Christ in you, the hope of glory." (Colossians 1:27)

It's difficult to love others when our feelings are involved. I know that sounds strange to some because they may think one needs feelings to "fall" in love. However, if it's possible to "fall" in love, it stands to reason; a person can "fall" out of love. True love, which is God's love doesn't fall in or out. Love is not determined by falling; it's demonstrated through faith. And through faith, love never fails.

God always commands our will to act and not our emotions to feel.

"This is my commandment, that ye love one another, as I have loved you." (John 15:12)

Jesus, a friend of publicans and sinners went home with Zacchaeus.

"And when Jesus came to the place, he looked up, and saw him, and said unto him, Zacchaeus, make haste, and come down; for today I must abide at thy house." (Luke 19:5)

Jesus chose to go to Zacchaeus' house not because of His feelings. Everything He did was based upon His obedience to the Father's will. This is not to say Jesus didn't love Zacchaeus. Jesus loves us all. He is full of love. And His love compelled Him to reach Zacchaeus.

Likewise, we cannot be afraid to reach out with the love of God to people that are different from us. We are to love them with God's love.

"Beloved, if God so loved us, we ought also to love one another." (1st John 4:11)

The Father's love is an act of our will. If we have the foundation of agape love then all the other expressions of love (*eros, storge and phileo*) are incorporated in us.

For those of us who are married; during the wedding ceremony the word *feeling* was not included anywhere in our vows. The preacher said, "***Will*** you take this man or woman to be your lawfully wedded husband or wife?" Although strong feelings may be present on the wedding day, the vows are not based on feelings. Marriage is an act of our will.

"Husbands love your wives, even as Christ also loved the church, and gave himself for it." (Ephesians 5:25)

A man was talking to his pastor and said, "I don't love my wife anymore." The pastor reminded the man, "The Bible says love your neighbor." The man stated emphatically, "I can't stand the woman, I hate her." The pastor then replied, "Well the Bible declares: love your enemy!"

Beloved, there is no way to get out or around it; we have to love one another. Someone might gripe: "What's the point?" Well, the point is our love for Jesus. If we love Jesus we won't allow something as small as our feelings to get in the way of loving others for Him. When we love Jesus, we operate from His agape love and we are not dominated by our feelings.

Those who love only from a point of feelings have a love that is narrow and shallow. A *narrow love* conveys: "I only love those who love me." A *shallow love* displays: "I only greet and give to those who greet and give to me."

What difference will our love make if we only love those who love us; greet those who greet us; and only give to those who give to us? Are we any different from the world?

God declared:

> *"For mine house shall be called an house of prayer for all people."* (Isaiah 56:7b)

It was God's grace that covered us in our sins. The darkness has passed and the true light is now shining in our lives. That light is the light of love. We must now walk in the light of God's love. The Lord is saying to all of us, "*Give me your heart and I will show you how to love people you don't like.*"

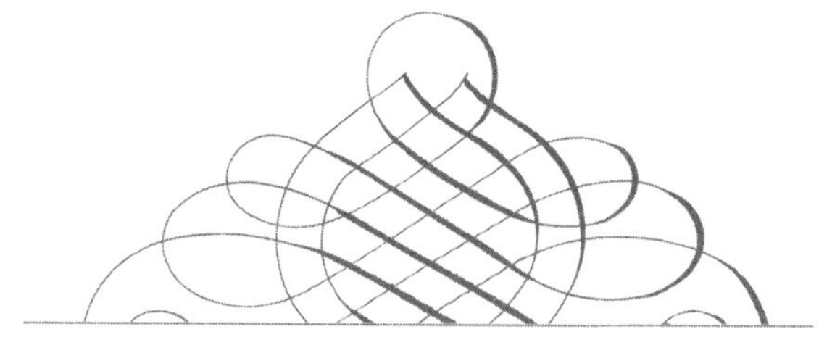

THE INGREDIENT OF LOVE
JOY

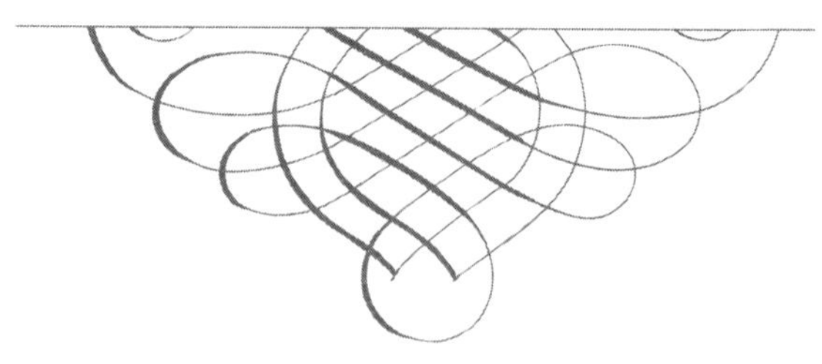

5

JOY IS LOVE'S STRENGTH

*"But the fruit of the spirit is love, **joy**..."*
(GALATIANS 5:22 BOLDNESS ADDED)

The fruit of the spirit is love and the first manifestation of love is joy. Joy is an inside job; meaning we have to have joy on the inside because it's not found on the outside. Joy is different from the happiness of the world.

The world does not have joy. The world has happiness that originates from an old Anglo Saxon word *happenstance*, where we get our English word *circumstance*; meaning if things aren't happening the way we want them to happen there goes our happiness.

If we are to have joy it must derive from knowing God loves us. Jesus gave His life to show His undying love. Therefore, we should live with a jubilant disposition. Whether in harmony or hardship we rejoice because we have Jesus and He's the answer to humanity's problems.

—JOY COMES FROM THE LORD—

Dr. A.L. Patterson notes: "Joy is a deep sense of an inner well-being that is *independent* of outward circumstances." Joy knows the Lord has adequate resources to handle whatever problems we face.

> *"...For this day is holy unto our Lord: neither be ye sorry; for the* ***joy of the LORD is your strength.****"*
> (Nehemiah 8:10 boldness added)

Joy is the Christian's strength. It allows us to have a deep sense of an inner wellbeing that is independent of negative circumstances. We have to be independent of the world so that we can be dependent on the Lord; dependent on our God and the power of His Christ. Through joy we are reminded: *It is not by might, nor by power, but by the Spirit of the living God* (Zech. 4:6).

Through joy we understand the Lord has adequate resources to handle life's problems. When we can do nothing; the Lord is able to do anything. This is how we as believing Believers can lift up our hands. We are able to praise the living God because we have "*joy unspeakable and it's full of glory* (1st Pet. 1:8)."

Paul is incarcerated, yet he says, *"Rejoice in the Lord always* (Phil. 4:4)."Let's examine the word "rejoice." The prefix *re* means do it over again. We cannot *rejoice* if we have no *joy*. However, if we have joy we can re-joice.

We can find joy again and again when we understand who we have in the Lord. The exciting thing about the Lord is encapsulated in these six words: *Who He is; I am His.* There's nothing like knowing we're loved by God. We can find joy believing in Jesus; we can keep joy knowing we belong to Him. When we rejoice in the Lord, our identity is in His divinity. If we are confused about who He is; rejoicing becomes difficult.

When Moses was called by God to deliver the children of Israel, He asked, "Who am I going to tell them sent me (Ex. 3:13)?" God gave Moses a class on His identity. God could have started with *Elohim*, the God of creation and restoration. He's the God in the beginning. He could have started there, but He didn't.

He could have answered with *El Elyon*, the Most High God, the possessor of heaven and earth. He decided not to. He could have rehearsed that He is *El Roi*, the God that sees and watches over all. Still, that wasn't sufficient enough.

He could have answered Moses by saying that He is *El Shaddai*, the God of the much more who makes all grace abound towards us, so that we always have all sufficiency in all things. Instead, He said, "*I AM.*"

Moses must have thought, "I am what?" Moses understood God's statement was incomplete. Therefore, God said, tell them *"I AM THAT I AM* (Ex. 3:14)*." I AM* is translated in Hebrew as *Jehovah. Jehovah* is a compound name. Moses mistook God's statement as incomplete, but actually nothing about God is incomplete. In essence, God gave Israel reasons to rejoice.

I AM is as complete a statement as God could give. Only God can claim "I Am" and stand correct and complete. Actually,

God was declaring, if they are lost; tell them *I AM The Way.* If they are philosophers; tell them *I AM The Truth.* If they are astrologists; tell them *I AM The Bright* and *Morning Star.* If they are geologists; tell them *I AM The Rock* of all ages, and *The Rock* in a weary land. To the gardener, *I AM The Rose of Sharon* and *The Lily* of the valleys; to the baker, *I AM The Bread of Life* which comes down from heaven; to the jeweler, *I AM The Pearl* of great price; to the sick, *I AM The Great Physician*; to the troubled, *I AM The Great Advocate*; to the soldier, *I AM The Captain* of the Lord's host and to the sinner, *I AM The Savior.* In other words, whatever the need, tell them to fill in the blank—that's who *I AM!* Above all, *I Am Love* (1st Jhn. 4:8). And that's more than enough!

Love is a many splendored thing. Therefore, rejoice in the Lord always (Phil. 4:4).

—JOY: THE KEY TO VICTORY—

To rejoice is the key to victory in any difficulty. In order to have joy exercised there must be trouble. Apart from trouble, we're left with happiness.

There's a sense of excitement to receive a paycheck, but that is not joy. The test of joy is when a paycheck is expected, but there isn't one. The seasoned saints use to say, "Don't wait 'til the battle is over; shout now!"

The next time we're confronted with negative situations we need to rejoice. This will confuse the devil. Baffled, the devil will ask, "Why are they rejoicing?" With confidence we can tell him, "*That's for nothing, wait until you do something*!" The adversary doesn't comprehend how we can have joy in the midst of pain because he doesn't love. God's love assures us no matter the difficulty, in spite the danger; we can remain strong through joy. Joy is love's strength. It allows us to face off with the devil and defeat him every time.

We are being perfected in the love of God when we rejoice. To claim our victory our resolve must be, "This joy that I have the world didn't give it to me and the world can't take it away!" Even in the midst of crying with tears coming down our faces, we can rejoice. We can still shout hallelujah and give God glory. Victory shall be ours because joy is the key.

Tough times don't last, but tough people do. Joy allows us to be strong and outlast any crisis. In the tough times, let joy come out. The devil brings trials to get us out of Christ's character. However, we must hold our peace, and let the Lord fight our battles, victory is already ours!

The word of the Lord, declared by Moses was:

> "*...Fear ye not, stand still, and see the salvation of the LORD, which he will shew to you to day: for the Egyptians whom ye have seen to day, ye shall see them again no more forever.*" (Exodus 14:13)

The joy of the Lord is our strength. God is working out what we cannot figure out. God is making the crooked thing straight. God is saying to stay in His love and let joy come out.

The anointing comes upon us when we can express the joy of the Lord. Once the anointing comes upon us, it *removes the burdens and destroys the yoke* (Isa. 10:27).

This is why David said, "*I will bless the Lord at all times and His praise shall continually be in my mouth* (Psa. 34:1)." Praise is comely (Psa. 33:1), meaning it makes us look better; it makes us feel better. Deep down on the inside God is working it out while we are praising, magnifying and glorifying Him.

When Jehoshaphat was notified that three armies had united and were on their way to besiege and destroy the nation of Israel, he prayed unto God. God gave the answer to their deliverance which was to allow Judah (*Praise*) to go first and lead the way (2nd Chr. 20:21).

Praise is related to joy and joy is our strength. The Lord told Jehoshaphat the battle was not Israel's, the battle was His. Thus, by the time Jehoshaphat and Israel arrived to the battlefield the fight was over. Consequently, they spent three days picking up spoils from the warfare (2nd Chr. 20:25).

Joy gives us the strength we need to endure any challenge. We will not maintain joy without experiencing the love of God the Father.

James the Apostle said:

> "*My brethren, count it all joy when ye fall into divers temptations.*" (James 1:2)

The word joy from the preceding passage is the Greek word "*chara*."[18] This joy carries the meaning of inner gladness; a depth of assurance and confidence that ignites a cheerful and rejoicing heart that leads to cheerful and rejoicing behavior. In the midst of trouble, trauma, and trials, we can count it all joy because this will bring us victory.

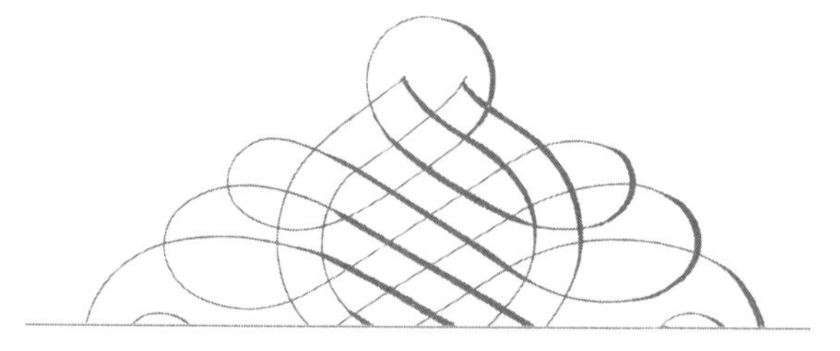

THE INGREDIENT OF LOVE
PEACE

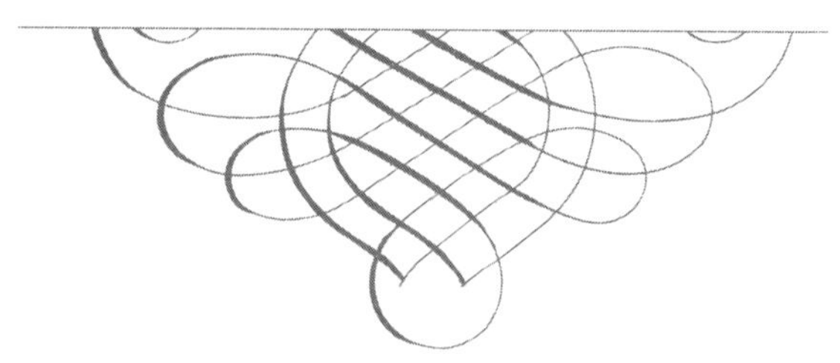

6

PEACE IS LOVE'S SAFETY

"But the fruit of the spirit is love, joy, ***peace...****"*

(GALATIANS 5:22 BOLDNESS ADDED)

Paul encouraged the hearts of the saints at Philippi when he described a harmonious relationship between God and man. This relationship is marked by peace.

> *"And the peace of God, which passeth all understanding, shall keep your hearts and minds through Christ Jesus."* (Philippians 4:7)

The word peace is the Greek word, *"eirene."*[19] Eirene further defined, is a deep sense of an inner well-being, *undisturbed* by outward circumstances. This means we are not disturbed when events occur contrary to our desires.

Love is a many splendored thing and because God's love is shed abroad in our hearts we can have peace beyond our comprehension. This means in spite of negative circumstances God's love makes us feel safe.

Those who faithfully follow Jesus discover He can calm

raging seas, walk on water and move mountains. Sure the Lord is mighty; moreover, His love is magnificent. His love causes Him to heal those who hurt and empower those who are helpless.

—The Lord Is Our Peace—

Spiritually speaking, if man does not have peace with God, he will not be at peace with himself. If he is not at peace with himself, he cannot be at peace with others. God's love acts as His peace treaty. It assures us we are safe and reminds us we are the apple of His eye.

It's imperative we have and maintain a harmonious relationship with God. A heart unoccupied by Jesus will result in a mind occupied with disturbing thoughts.

Peace is not just something; it's Someone. The Lord Himself is our peace. He's a Rock in a weary land; a sure foundation in uncertain times. The Lord does not merely give us peace; He's the very peace we need.

Gideon was troubled because God had assigned him to fight against the Midianites (Judg. 6). Fearful of the outcome, Gideon explained to God that he was the least of everybody in his family, and that his family was the least in all of Israel!

In spite of Gideon's perception of Himself and the circumstances he faced, God called him a mighty man of valor. Then God revealed Himself to Gideon as "*Jehovah Shalom, the Lord who is my peace* (Judg. 6:24)."

It is essential that we understand peace is not just something;

it's *Someone* who gives us something! Jesus is God's peace personified, and the extension of God's love. It's His job to keep us in perfect peace; it's our job to keep our minds on Him.

> *"And above all these things put on charity, which is the bond of perfectness. And let the* ***peace of God*** *rule in your hearts, to the which also ye are called in one body; and be ye thankful."* (Colossians 3:14-15 boldness added)

The Amplified Bible reads:

> *"And let the peace (soul harmony which comes) from Christ rule (act as umpire continually) in your hearts (deciding and settling with finality all questions that arise in your minds, in that peaceful state)..."* (Colossians 3:15 AMP)

If we were to liken life to a game of baseball, we would be the players, but the Lord alone stands as the Umpire. As the pitcher, the devil throws all kinds of stuff our way. He may throw a fast ball (something too soon), or a curve ball (something unexpected), but we're empowered by God's Spirit to hit the devil's stuff every time.

As we run the bases, first, second and third, we turn the corner sprinting for home plate. Whether we stroll into home or slide, Jesus as our Umpire declares—safe! He brings our soul into harmony (home) with God. Peace is loves safety and it declares we are safe even though trouble is all around us.

Where is the safest place on earth? The safest place is in the love of God. We are told to keep ourselves in God's love (Jude 21) because there we will find His blessings, peace and safety.

The Bible records:

"He that dwelleth in the secret place of the most High shall abide under the shadow of the Almighty. I will say of the Lord, He is my refuge and my fortress: my God; in him will I trust." (Psalm 91:1-2)

It is Jesus who keeps us safe under the canopy of His protection. A harmonious relationship with God creates for us a harmonious relationship with man, and this provides the peace in our hearts.

"And let the peace (soul harmony which comes) from Christ rule (act as umpire continually) in your hearts [deciding and settling with finality all questions that arise in your minds, in that peaceful state]..." (Colossians 3:15 AMP)

—The Lord Gives Us Peace—

*"Now **the Lord of peace himself give you peace** always by all means. The Lord be with you all."*
(2nd Thessalonians 3:16 boldness added)

The Lord is *Jehovah Shalom* who is our peace and who gives us peace under all circumstances by any means necessary! There is nothing too hard for the Lord!

*"Thou wilt keep him in **perfect peace**, whose mind is stayed on thee: because he trusteth in thee."* (Isaiah 26:3 boldness added)

In the aforementioned passage, the phrase *perfect peace* is also translated as "*shalom.*"[20] This is the same word found in Judges 6:24. *Shalom* carries the meaning of completeness; welfare and health. *Shalom* further speaks to a harmonious state of the soul and mind.

Shalom is the state of being at ease internally regardless of what happens externally.

In the Hebrew tradition, *shalom* is also expressed in the phrase *beshalom*, "*in peace*."[21]

> "*I will both lay me down in peace, and sleep: for thou, Lord, only makest me dwell in safety.*" (Psalm 4:8)

Isaiah prophesied of Jesus' incarnation as the "*Prince of Peace*" whose kingdom was to introduce a government of "*peace*" (Isa. 9:6-7).

The Scripture records:

> "***For He is our peace,*** *who hath made both one, and hath broken down the middle wall of partition between us.*" (Ephesians 2:14 boldness added)

Jesus came to break down the wall in order to repair the relationship between the Nation of Israel and the Gentiles or non-Jewish nations. Jesus as our peace has broken barriers that once separated us. It is not God's desire for us to be separated but rather His desire is that we be one.

> "*Having abolished in his flesh the enmity, even the law of commandments contained in ordinances; for to make in himself of* ***twain one new man, so making peace.***" (Ephesians 2:15 boldness added)

Jesus' goal is to take two separate groups, place them together and make them one. In His high priestly prayer, He communicated the Father's heart:

> *"And now I am no more in the world, but these are in the world, and I come to thee. Holy Father, keep through thine own name those whom thou hast given me, that* ***they may be one, as we are."*** (John 17:11 boldness added)

Jesus serves as an umpire making us one with the Father, pronouncing us safe, and He also serves as a *peacemaker.* When we have God as the peacemaker inside us, we become peacemakers.

Love is a many splendored thing. It compels us to be at peace with others and is the source and sign we belong to God.

The Bible states:

> *"Blessed are the peacemakers: for they shall be called the children of God."* (Matthew 5:9)

The Lord through the Prophet Ezekiel declared:

> *"Moreover I will make a* ***covenant of peace*** *with them; it shall be an everlasting covenant with them: and I will place them, and multiply them, and will set my sanctuary in the midst of them for evermore. My tabernacle also shall be with them: yea, I will be their God, and they shall be my people."* (Ezekiel 37:26-27 boldness added)

In essence, Ezekiel prophesied of the fulfillment and completion; entering into a state of wholeness and unity; a restoration of a harmonious relationship between God and man because Jesus is the peacemaker!

> "And came and ***preached peace*** to you which were afar off, and to them that were nigh." (Ephesians 2:17 boldness added)

Jesus came and preached peace! He then granted us access to God the Father with the possibility of war between God and man ending. Peace is love's safety. There would be no way for us to come to God without His love creating the path.

> *"For through him we both have access by one Spirit unto the Father."* (Ephesians 2:18)

Vine's Expository Dictionary of Old and New Testament Words translates the word "access" in this passage as *"prosagoge." Prosagoge* means *"a leading or bringing into the presence of."* This is to say Jesus doesn't send us to the Father; He takes us to the Father. His peace guards our hearts and He guides us with His love.

The peace Jesus brings gives us a deep sense of inner well-being, that is undisturbed by outward circumstances. By this, no weapon formed against us shall prosper. There is nothing that can interrupt our peace.

It is the Lord Jesus Christ, the Prince of Peace who leads us into the presence of the Father. Now that we are at peace with God, we can have peace with ourselves and everybody else.

Love is a many splendored thing. Therefore, we must keep ourselves in God's love. In His love we find stability, security and above all else, peace which is love's safety.

THE INGREDIENT OF LOVE
LONGSUFFERING

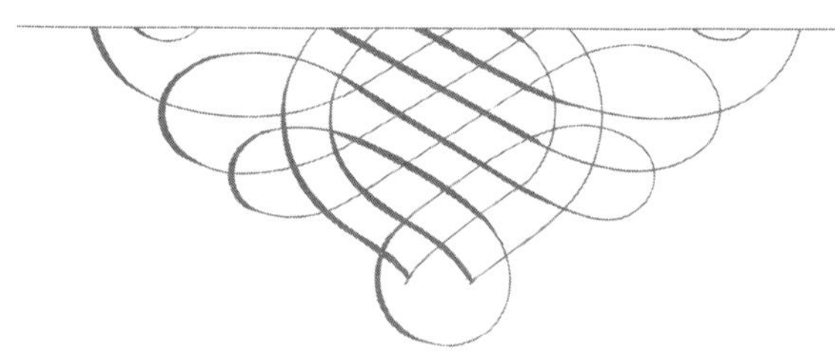

LONGSUFFERING IS LOVE'S PATIENCE

*"But the fruit of the spirit is love, joy, peace, **long suffering**..."*
(GALATIANS 5:22 BOLDNESS ADDED)

People exercise to stay strong. I am referring to the rigorous training we place on our muscles. We work out to get strength and to stay in shape. Various weights give strength to our muscles. And, just as weights give strength to muscles, love provides strength to the man. Love's pathway to making people strong is through longsuffering. Longsuffering is love's patience.

Longsuffering is another side of love we must develop and display. It is critical for us to handle life and help people, because love is a many splendored thing!

—Strength Is For Service—

Romans 15:1 of the Message Bible reads: *"Strength is for service."* Some stay weak because they do not serve God or anyone else. Why would God give us strength if we are not going to serve? *"...Strength is for service, not status...* (Rom. 15:1 MSG)."

Let us consider two verses of scripture. Romans 15:1 states: *"We then that are strong..."* However, Romans 14:1 records: *"Him that is weak..."* These scriptures indicate that there are strong and weak Christians; strong and weak people.

Romans 15:1 also declares: *"We then that are strong are to bear..."* The word bear in this passage means to forebear; put up with; keep stretching out or to remain longsuffering. So then the scripture can be interpreted: "*We then that are strong* (are to display longsuffering or) *bear the infirmities of the weak."*

The word, "infirmities," implies weakness. It could also imply a person is sick causing them to become weak. So Paul says, *"We then that are strong ought to bear the infirmities of the weak, and not to please ourselves."*

As a pastor I have been partaker of the principle *bearing the infirmities of the weak.* My title as a pastor does not entitle me to special treatment from others; rather it demands I treat others special. This is not hard when I remember the Lord has delivered me from my infirmities and has given me strength in His Son Jesus.

Again, longsuffering deals with patience. The Bible connotes, first there is the natural afterwards is the spiritual (1st Cor. 15:46). When an officer enters into the U. S. Army, they do not begin their military career as a General. They must climb the steps of the Army's rank structure—2nd Lieutenant, 1st Lieutenant, Captain, Major, etc. In other words, you do not start off at the top.

Many are impatient, and cannot condescend to men of a lower state. It's difficult to condescend if you've never started from the bottom. Some have titles, but no substance. Some desire titles to impress, but are not willing to help others.

God desires us to be helpful. He loves us and His love allows us to love others. When we love like God loves, we will be longsuffering. We'll seek opportunities to serve. We'll find ways to help the less fortunate. Also, we'll extend patience whenever it's needed.

—Longsuffering Bears People—

"Each one of us needs to look after the good of the people around us, asking ourselves, "How can I help?" (Romans 15:2 MSG)

A weak person is looking for someone who can help them. The person of strength asks "How can I help; how can I serve?" A weak person has their hand out; a person of strength is quick to lend a helping hand. Now, I'm not advocating we should never look for assistance, because everyone at some point needs help. However, I am making the distinction of a person who lives in the state of weakness or strength. The weak person suffers long; meaning they see no resolution, no recovery. The person of strength is longsuffering. They experience pain, but allow patience and love to provide strength.

The word longsuffering in Galatians 5:22 is the Greek word "*makrothumia*."[22] It carries the connotation of enduring long with people, not problems. Primarily, we need patience for projects, problems or predicaments. We need longsuffering for people. The word "*makrothumia*" is used to describe how to respond to people you have to put up with.

Longsuffering carries the understanding of a woman carrying a baby for nine months. There is a season, and a due date. The expected mother is excited and delighted. Nevertheless, she has to suffer long. She endures agony and suffers as her body stretches. In one sense, there is a delight but in another, there is no pleasure. This mother and child experience becomes the first of many lessons of how to be longsuffering with people. Likewise, our assignment of longsuffering means caring for people full term.

Barnabas, whose name means "son of encouragement" was an instrument of God's love and an example of longsuffering (*makrothumia*). He displayed longsuffering towards his beloved brother Paul.

> *"And some days after Paul said unto Barnabas, Let us go again and visit our brethren in every city where we have preached the word of the Lord, and see how they do.*
>
> *And Barnabas determined to take with them John, whose surname was Mark. But Paul thought not good to take him with them, who departed from them from Pamphylia, and went not with them to the work.*
>
> ***And the contention was so sharp between them**, that they departed asunder one from the other: and so Barnabas took Mark, and sailed unto Cyprus; And Paul chose Silas, and*

> *departed, being recommended by the brethren unto the grace of God."* (Acts 15:36-40 boldness added)

The phrase "the contention was so sharp" in the previous passage is translated as "*paroxusmos*."[23] The idea of this encounter in the original Greek is that of differing to the point of suffering pain.

Contrary to the impression usually painted of this particular conflict between Barnabas and Paul; the scene portrays the idea both men were grieved and distressed.

Their differences were sharp. The hearts of both men were cut deeply over their differing positions concerning Mark. This does not mean they were cutting each other with sharp and ugly words. It's just their opposing convictions cut to the point of separation. They loved and respected each other, and their *sharp* conflict seemed irreconcilable. There seemed to be no solution other than to depart from each other. Paul took Silas with him, and Barnabas took Mark.

Paul's last epistle, written from a Roman jail cell, was to Timothy his spiritual son who happened to be a pastor. He wrote: "*But watch thou in all things, endure afflictions, do the work of an evangelist, make full proof of thy ministry* (2nd Tim. 4:5)."

The letter went on to say:

> *"For Demas hath forsaken me, having loved this present world, and is departed unto Thessalonica; Crescens to Galatia, Titus unto Dalmatia. Only Luke is with me.* ***Take Mark, and bring him with thee for he is profitable to me for the ministry."*** (2nd Timothy 4:10-11 boldness added)

At first Paul deemed Mark unfit for the work in the ministry. How did Mark become profitable to Paul after the sharp contention of Acts 15? Mark was profitable because Barnabas was *longsuffering.*

Love allowed Barnabas to remain longsuffering with Mark and to see what others could not see in the beginning—he was profitable. Think of how many people we may have given up on because we failed to see them through the eyes of God. God's love expands our hearts to become longsuffering with people others have given up on. We must be willing to carry those weights that may hinder them from moving forward. Love is a many splendored thing!

The Word of God records we have fulfilled the law of Christ if we bear one another's burdens (Gal. 6:2). Notice, the word burden in the preceding scripture is plural. This means we are to carry more than just our own burden. The Greek word for *burdens* is "*baros*" which means weight, load, or a demand on your resources.[24]

The Apostle Paul says: *"For every man shall bear his own burden* (Gal. 6:5)." Notice, the word burden here is singular. Again, *burdens* refers to weight; but *burden* is the Greek word *phortion*, or portion. In essence, "Let everyman bear *his own* portion."[25]

Many people in church have burdens (weights) because some people in church are not bearing their own burden (portion). God wants us to be developed and disciplined to carry our share. And we must be dependable to suffer long with others. This takes possessing the patience of God.

—Longsuffering Bears Patience—

"But let patience have her perfect work, that ye may be perfect and entire, wanting nothing." (James 1:4)

Another aspect of longsuffering is patience.

Longsuffering which is love's patience is for God's glory, others gain and our growth. It is God's desire that we grow and mature in the nature and quality of longsuffering.

"My brethren, count it all joy when you fall into divers temptations; Knowing this, that the trying of your faith worketh patience." (James 1:2-3)

The word for patience in the preceding passage is "*hupomone.*" In its literal meaning *hupomone* is not passive; it is active.[26] Patience (*hupomone*) stands up and faces the trials of life. *Hupomone* is the quality and caliber of life that does not surrender to circumstances or succumb under pressure. When trials or trouble pushes us in a corner, patience takes position and says, *"I got your back!"*

We must always remember God loves us unconditionally. When we focus on God's love we can have patience through any storm. God's love grants longsuffering which in turn allows us to patiently wait for God's results.

"And he shall speak great words against the most High, and shall ***wear out the saints of the most High****, and think to change times and laws..."* (Daniel 7:25 boldness added)

The Believer must understand, patience is the force of consistency causing us to remain constant and always the same. Instead of the devil wearing us out, we end up wearing him out.

Patience allows us to go through a difficult situation without giving God a timeline to get us out. It is at this point that *hupomone,* teaches us how to wait on the Lord.

> *"He giveth power to the faint; and to them that have no might he increaseth strength. Even the youths shall faint and be weary, and the young men shall utterly fall: But they that wait upon the LORD shall renew their strength; they shall mount up with wings as eagles; they shall run, and not be weary; and they shall walk, and not faint."* (Isaiah 40:29-31)

God loves His people and desires that we endure through many hardships. We must show the world our God can create light where there is darkness, life where there is death, and certainly patience through longsuffering. God's love allows us to serve the weak because we possess His strength. Remember, God is not on a timeline, but He is always on time with His love because love is a many splendored thing.

THE INGREDIENT OF LOVE
GENTLENESS

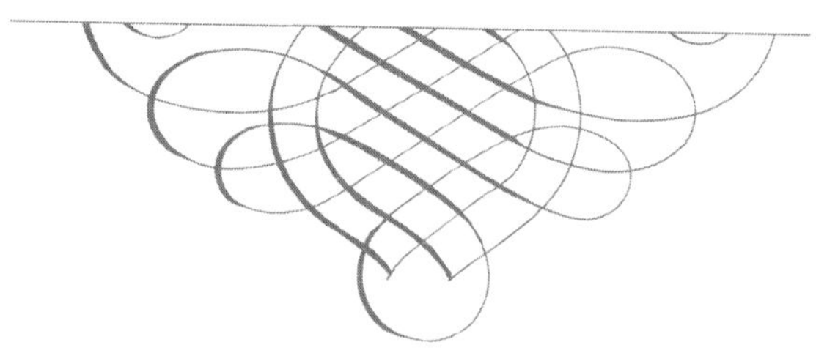

8

GENTLENESS IS LOVE'S CONDUCT

"But the fruit of the spirit is love, joy, peace, long suffering, ***gentleness...****"*

(GALATIANS 5:22 BOLDNESS ADDED)

Like a kaleidoscope love can be seen from many spectrums. Let's view love through gentleness. Gentleness is the virtue of love that is kind, caring, and sharing. As love's conduct, gentleness is compassion in action.

> *"But when he saw the multitudes, he was moved with compassion on them, because they fainted, and were scattered abroad, as sheep having no shepherd."* (Matthew 9:36)

This word compassion means to "*be moved inwardly; to yearn with tender mercy, affection, pity, and empathy.*"[27] Jesus saw the crowds fainting, under the stress and direst of sickness and disease both spiritually and physically (vs.35).

The multitude was weary in body and soul. Jesus saw them "scattered abroad as sheep without a shepherd." He saw the multitude as sighing, crying and dying. Therefore, He was moved with love's conduct—gentleness. Gentleness is compassion in action.

—COMPASSION IN ACTION—

The gentle person simply loves people and loves peace. Therefore, the gentle person walks humbly among men regardless of their status and circumstances in life.

> *"And the servant of the Lord must not strive; but be gentle unto all men, apt to teach, patient."* (2nd Timothy 2:24)

In the following passage the Apostle Paul will combine the qualities of meekness and gentleness. Meekness and gentleness are synonymous qualities of love's conduct. Meekness means to be gentle, tender, humble, mild, considerate, but with strength. Meekness has the strength to control with discipline, and it does so at the right time.

> *"Now I Paul myself beseech you by the meekness and gentleness of Christ, who in presence am base among you, but being absent am bold toward you."* (2nd Corinthians 10:1)

The Lord says through the Prophet Isaiah:

> *"...Surely they are My people, sons who will not lie [who will not deal falsely with Me]; and so He was to them a Savior [in all their distresses]. In all their affliction He was afflicted, and the Angel of His presence saved them; in His love and in His pity He redeemed them..."* (Isaiah 63:8-9a AMP)

God was moved with compassion for His people and the "*Angel of His presence*" saved them!

Luke gives a compelling account of a paralyzed man. His friends took him to be healed of Jesus. The crowd prohibited them from entering the door of the house where Jesus was ministering. Yet, they were not discouraged or deterred. These determined men lowered their paralyzed partner through the roof of the house.

What was it that caused these men to go to such lengths on behalf of their disabled friend? The answer is in the latter portion of Luke 5:17: "*And the power of the Lord was present to heal them.*"

Where there's the presence of the Lord, love's conduct, which is compassion in action, is present! It was their faith in Jesus, and the love they had for their friend that moved them to act. Love's conduct is compassion in action.

There's nothing we won't do for those in need when we have the love of the Father in us. We must keep ourselves in the love of God. It's when we're in His love we can reach others and cause them to reach Jesus Christ. Like the men who brought their friend to Jesus, we'll bring people to Him no matter the cost.

Gentleness is the key. Gentleness attracts people of every ethnicity. It removes barriers that would otherwise remain. God has been gentle by providing us with His Spirit. When we were enemies of God and rejected His will for our lives, His Spirit gently approached and told us that God was our Father (Rom. 8:15). God captured us not by a firm grip, but a gentle touch.

The greatest account in the Bible on how to display compassion in action is the Good Samaritan (Lu. 10:30-37). After Jesus advised His audience to love their neighbor, a lawyer asked, "Who is my neighbor?" Without hesitation Jesus shared the following account: a certain man went down from Jerusalem to Jericho and met misfortune by the hands of thieves. The thieves roughed up and robbed the man then left him for dead.

A priest who was a Jew saw his fellow Jew but had no compassion. Then there was a Levite, a church leader who passed the injured man. In our day and time he would be a pastor or a deacon. He also failed to show concern.

Then a Samaritan man came upon the wounded Jew. In those days Jews and Samaritans shared mutual contempt for one another. However, this Samaritan had compassion and provided care for a stranger—an enemy, because love is a many splendored thing!

—A GENTLE SERVANT—

> *"And the servant of the Lord must not be quarrelsome (fighting and contending). Instead, he must be kindly to everyone* and *mild-tempered [preserving the bond of peace]; he must be a skilled* and *suitable teacher, patient* and *forbearing* and *willing to suffer wrong."* (2nd Timothy 2:24 AMP)

The word gentle in the King James Version of the aforementioned text is translated as "*epios*," which means "*mild* or *kind*."[28] Vine's Expository Dictionary of Old and New Testament Words defines gentleness as: "*conduct requisite for a servant of the Lord*."

James the brother of our Lord introduced himself in his

epistle as "*A **servant** of God and of the Lord Jesus Christ* (Jam. 1:1)." If anyone could have gloated or ridden the coattail of Jesus, certainly it could have been His brother. Rather than boasting in his family status as the Lord's brother, James chose to firmly state his position as the Lord's servant. The term James chose in the original Greek for our English word servant is "*doulos.*"

Vine's Expository Dictionary of Old and New Testament Words translates *doulos* as a bondman, one that is bound, or a slave. Originally, this was the lowest term in the scale of servitude, which also came to mean "*one who gives himself up to the will of another.*"

It is from this position of servitude that James declared:

> *"But the wisdom that is from above is first pure, then peaceable,* ***gentle****, and easy to be intreated, full of mercy and good fruits, without partiality, and without hypocrisy."* (James 3:17 boldness added)

The Apostle James, in defining and discussing the nature of *wisdom that is from above,* provided instruction and understanding of the core attributes of wisdom that include gentleness. The Word of God declares: "He that wins souls is wise" (Prov. 11:30). This is a true statement, but in order to win anyone you must be gentle. Jesus is the wisdom of God personified and He is "meek *(gentle)* and lowly (Matt. 11:29)."

Gentleness is love's conduct. Above all the descriptions Jesus could give of Himself, He chose to describe Himself as meek and lowly (Matt. 11:29). Jesus could have come to the world as a lion—He chose to be a lamb. He could have decided to swing the hammer of judgment—He received the nails of condemnation. He could have come triumphantly as the King—He entered quietly as a servant.

Gentleness doesn't demand its way; it makes a way for others. Gentleness is compassion in action. Jesus is the expression of God's love. He was kind, caring and sharing.

To further qualify what it means to be a servant of the Lord, one that is kind, caring and sharing, we look to the account of Cain and Abel.

> *"And the LORD said unto Cain, Where is Abel thy brother? And he said, I know not: Am I my brother's keeper?"* (Genesis 4:9)

One of the qualifications of a servant is to keep our brother. Our brothers are kept through gentleness; showing concern for their welfare.

Cain's reaction to God's question was indicative of the fact that "*sin was no longer lying at the door* (vs.7)," sin had pounced on Cain and consumed him with murderous actions towards his brother. When we lose the love of God, sin is waiting to grip us. The imagery is of a panther waiting to pounce on its prey.

> *"And Cain talked with Abel his brother: and it came to pass, when they were in the field, that Cain rose up against Abel his brother, and slew him."* (Genesis 4:8)

It is imperative we understand that as gentle servants of the Lord, if we are not our brother's keepers, we can become our brother's killers!

—How May I Help—

> *"I look for someone to come and help me, but no one gives me a passing thought! No one will help me; no one cares a bit what happens to me."* (Psalm 142:4 NLT)

David was in great distress when he wrote the preceding passage. He was on the run from King Saul who at the time was deeply disturbed. Anyone assisting David was inviting Saul's wrath.

On one occasion Saul's son Jonathan, acted as an advocate for David. Saul's retort to Jonathan's pleas for David was life threatening (1st Sam. 20:33). Due to Saul's reaction to his own son, none of David's friends dared provide him any assistance. Thus, David lamented: *"I look for someone to come and help me, but no one gives me a passing thought! No one will help me; no one cares a bit what happens to me* (Psa. 142:4 NLT)."

No matter where we are in the world, there are people that are hurting. There are people who are battered, bruised, broken and are in need of love's conduct—gentleness. They need to see compassion in action.

> *"A bruised reed shall he not break, and a smoking flax shall he not quench, till he send forth judgment unto victory."* (Matthew 12:20)

Gentleness can be seen in the following analogy. Consider a beautiful flower garden. Imagine giving time and effort to cultivating it. However, while sleeping something comes in and threatens its beauty.

Perhaps a strong wind comes. It uproots trees, tosses shrubs, and bruises the flowers in the garden. Many would say it is easier to pull-up the bruised and bent and simply start anew.

However, with gentleness as love's conduct, Jesus shows compassion in action. He declares, "Through loving kindness, care and tenderness this bruised reed can live!" Some may insist, Lord it is easier to just tear this bruised reed up and get another one. The Lord says, "No, let it grow." His gentleness is imparted to us; His love is invested in us. Therefore, with compassion in action He saves us.

Due to the winds of adversity, many people are bruised and battered, but Jesus says, "Wait, I can mend you." At times we may feel broken into pieces, but the Father's love puts us together again. With gentleness and tenderness, Jesus makes us completely whole. Love is a many splendored thing!

Like the flicker and flame of a candle that's about to go out, Jesus declares, "I will not blow it out. There is still light!"

> *"He will not crush the weakest reed or put out a flickering candle."* (Matthew 12:20 NLT)

Although it may seem close to the end, where there is smoke, there is fire. Jesus proclaims, "I can breathe on it. I can bring it back—if there is smoke, there is still life."

Jesus can breathe new life upon a bruised reed. How does He do it? He does it with gentleness, with kindness, caring and sharing. The Lord is never through with us. Although the light may be diming, flickering here and there—Jesus can restore the flame.

> *"He won't walk over anyone's feelings, won't push you into a corner. Before you know it, his justice will triumph."* (Matthew 12:20 MSG)

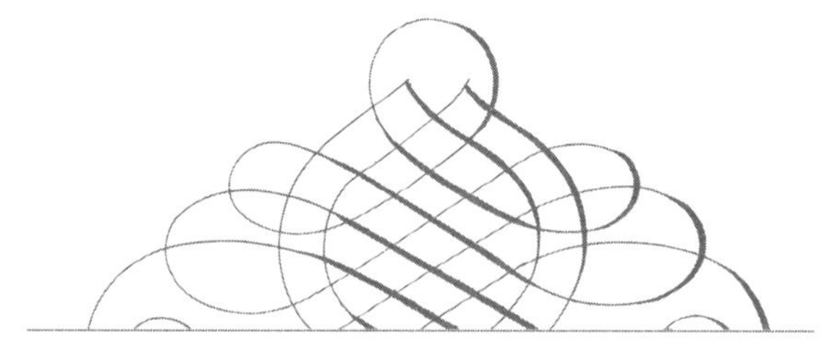

THE INGREDIENT OF LOVE
GOODNESS

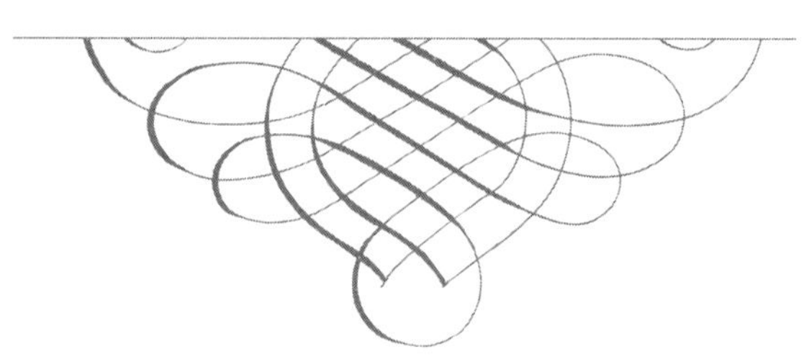

9

GOODNESS IS LOVE'S CHARACTER

*"But the fruit of the spirit is love, joy, peace, long suffering, gentleness, **goodness**..."*

(GALATIANS 5:22 BOLDNESS ADDED)

The fruit of the spirit is the character or nature of God's love (Gal. 5:22-23). Out of love derives joy, peace, longsuffering, gentleness and the subject of this chapter, *goodness*. Goodness is love's character.

The Random House Dictionary defines character as "*the aggregate of features and traits that form the individual nature of a person or thing.*" A person with character thrives to be good.

Whatever we do should stem from the goodness of God. In other words, we should operate out of the love of God personified in the Lord Jesus Christ (1st John 4:8). W.E. Vines Expository Dictionary of Old and New Testament Words translates the trilogy of the word good.

This trilogy begins with *Agathos,* which is good in its character and beneficial in its effect; the second component is *Euarestos,* which connotes something that is well pleasing; and the third component of the trilogy is *Teleios*, which means to *bring to full development, growth, and maturity.*

All three definitions reveal "good" as beneficial, pleasing and instrumental for our growth. One of the greatest discoveries we can make is that Jesus is good for our lives.

—Jesus Is Good for Us—

The first thing that needs to be established is the fact, Jesus is good for us. Again, for something to be considered good (agathos) it must be good in its character and beneficial in its effect. This definition is certainly befitting of Jesus.

Jesus is good for us because in Him is the light, life and love of God. Love is a many splendored thing. The greatest experience we can have is the love God gives. As God's love personified Jesus said:

> *"...I am the light of the world: he that followeth me shall not walk in darkness, but shall have the light of life."* (John 8:12)

Some people live in perpetual spiritual darkness. It seems that everywhere we look things are dismal and darkened with hopelessness. In spite of this dim state, Jesus is our light. He is our Savior and He is good for us.

There are many sinners, but only one Savior. Romans 3:23 reminds us, *"All have sinned and come short of the glory of God."* Let's state the obvious, every sinner needs a Savior. We need a Savior who loves us and is good for us, and Jesus is the only One who fits that bill.

No one else claimed to be the Savior. Mohammad did not claim to be the Savior. He claimed to be a prophet. Confucius did not claim to be the Savior. He claimed to be a philosopher. Some say Jesus was a prophet, others protested a philosopher. Nevertheless, God sent His messenger to proclaim that Jesus was the Savior.

> *"But while he thought on these things, behold, the angel of the Lord appeared unto him in a dream, saying, Joseph, thou son of David, fear not to take unto thee Mary thy wife: for that which is conceived in her is of the Holy Ghost. And she shall bring forth a son, and thou shalt call his name JESUS:* ***for he shall save his people from their sins."*** (Matthew 1:20-21 boldness added)

Vine's Expository Dictionary of Old and New Testament Words define the word "save" as "*sozo.*" *Sozo* is the spiritual and eternal salvation granted immediately by God to those who believe on the Lord Jesus Christ. *Sozo* is God's power to deliver from the bondage of sin.

Many are in bondage to their sin and have no strength by which to break the bonds. Jesus is God's love manifested to give us the strength we need. God will withhold no good thing from those who love Him.

> *"For God so loved the world, that he gave his only begotten Son, that whosoever believeth in him should not perish, but have everlasting life."* (John 3:16)

We need to understand, Jesus does not only have what we need; He is what we need.

God's people are like sheep, always in need of "The Shepherd." I think we all can agree a shepherd is absolutely good for sheep. Sheep are dumb and defenseless and it is the shepherd's duty to provide and protect the sheep. A cowboy drives cattle. A shepherd leads sheep. Jesus is a shepherd not a cowboy. He leads us to green pastures (Psalm 23:1-2).

The following passages allude to the three attributes of Jesus as our Shepherd. They reveal Him as the Good, Great and Chief Shepherd.

> *"I am the good shepherd: the **good shepherd** giveth his life for the sheep."* (John 10:11 boldness added)

The word great in the following scripture is translated in the original Greek as "*megas.*" The literal meaning of *megas is "the greatest.*"[29] The emphasis of the translation is that there is no greater shepherd than Jesus!

> *"Now the God of peace that brought again from the dead our Lord Jesus, that **great shepherd** of the sheep..."*
> (Hebrews 13:20 boldness added)

The Apostle Peter declares:

> *"And when the **Chief Shepherd** shall appear, ye shall receive a crown of glory that fadeth not away."*
> (1st Peter 5:4 boldness added)

Vine's translates chief in 1st Peter 5:4 as *"protos"* which denotes "*the first.*" As the Chief Shepherd, Jesus is the "Arch-shepherd" or "Archbishop" who is over all and to whom all shall give an account.[30]

Goodness as love's character is manifested in Jesus as our Good Shepherd, Great Shepherd and Chief Shepherd and He is good for us.

1. All sinners need a Savior—that's Jesus.
2. All sheep need a Shepherd—that's Jesus.
3. All souls need a Sovereign God—that's Jesus.

Jesus is our Sovereign King! He is Omniscient—He knows everything; He is Omnipresent—He is everywhere; and He is Omnipotent—He is all powerful. Above all else, He is love. Love is a many splendored thing! Jesus is good for us, so wherever we are He is there representing God's love.

> *"If I ascend up into heaven, thou art there: if I make my bed in hell, behold, thou art there. If I take the wings of the morning, and dwell in the uttermost parts of the sea; Even there shall thy hand lead me, and thy right hand shall hold me."*
> (Psalms 139: 8-10)

No matter where we are Jesus is there to embrace us with the love of God. The plot, ploy and plans of the enemy are to get us out of the love of God. Therefore, we know Jesus is good for us. Moreover, He is good in us.

—Jesus Is Good in Us—

> *"...Christ **in you** the hope of Glory."*
> (Colossians 1:27 boldness added)

Jesus *comes out* and is seen in our character if we *stay in* the love of God. My heart still burns with the love of God for; my wife, children, grandchildren, extended family and the church of the Lord Jesus Christ. My heart still burns with the love of God, for people in the world. When we stay in the love of God, Satan cannot touch the nature, or substance of this kind of love. We become too hot for the devil to handle!

Jesus said in Luke 4:18, "*The spirit of the Lord is upon me, and he hath anointed me...*" It is the anointing of God within us that removes burdens and destroys yokes (Isa. 10:27). This anointing compels us to entreat others with the love of God. It is paramount we get and keep Jesus in us. When Jesus is in us we can turn this upside down world right side up. His anointing empowers the church for the work in the earth (Matt. 28:19-20).

> *"Not forsaking the assembling of ourselves together, as the manner of some is; but exhorting one another: and so much the more, as ye see the day approaching."* (Hebrews 10:25)

As Christians, we need each other for fellowship, strength, encouragement, care, and love. In an expression of joy, David said, "*I was glad when they said unto me, Let us go into the house of the LORD* (Psa. 122:1)." David was glad to come to church. It is in coming to church that we learn of Jesus. It's all about Him!

Since Jesus is good in us we ought to appreciate and employ the quality of goodness more effectively. To do this let's explore the term good further.

Vine's Expository Dictionary of Old and New Testament Words translates the word good in Hebrew as "*tob.*" *Tob* carries the meaning as one who is *good*, or one who gives *delight* and *pleasure.*

The Theological Wordbook of the Old Testament further expands upon the meaning of *tob* as that which is "*practical or desirable, of quality and moral rightness.*"

In the book of Genesis, we are given the first lesson concerning goodness. It is at this juncture we learn the *Law of First Reference, or the Law of Primary – First Mention*. Genesis 1:10b is the first time God mentions the word good. Verses 12b, 18b, 21b and 25b all record the same phrase, "*And God saw that it was good.*" In verse 31 the Bible says, "*And God saw everything that he made, and it was **very** good.*" In each of these six Biblical references in Genesis chapter 1, good is translated as *tob*. When used of God it means the One who is *good*, or One who gives *delight* and *pleasure.*

When we allow Jesus to operate His goodness in us we are able to touch others and make a positive effect in their lives. We are able to bring delight where things are dim and turn situations from bad to good.

In our study of Genesis chapter 1, we learn that God made nothing bad. God made everything good! Some may ask why God made the devil, since he is bad. In reality, the devil *made himself* bad, just as people can make themselves bad.

The Bible speaking of Lucifer says:

> "*Thou wast perfect in thy ways from the day that thou wast created, till iniquity was found in thee.*" (Ezekiel 28:15)

Lucifer is a prime example to all. When God created Lucifer, he was an angel and perfect until iniquity was *found in him.*

Lucifer's account reveals what transpires when we close our hearts to the Lord:

> *"How art thou fallen from heaven, O Lucifer, son of the morning! how art thou cut down to the ground, which didst weaken the nations! For thou hast said in thine heart, I will ascend into heaven, I will exalt my throne above the stars of God: I will sit also upon the mount of the congregation, in the sides of the north: I will ascend above the heights of the clouds; I will be like the most High. Yet thou shalt be brought down to hell, to the sides of the pit."* (Isaiah 14:12-15)

Failure in submitting to God's love and Jesus' Spirit results in sin entering our lives. Sin is always upward against God. Transgression is always outward against others. Iniquity is that which is bent, twisted and wrong on the inside of one's self. God did not create Lucifer to fall. Lucifer made himself fall by sin, transgression and iniquity.

The Bible reminds us:

> *"For all that is in the world, the lust of the flesh, and the lust of the eyes, and the pride of life, is not of the Father, but is of the world."* (1st John 2:16)

We are further admonished:

> *"Moreover he must have a good report of them which are without; lest he fall into reproach and the snare of the devil."* (1st Timothy 3:7)

What is the snare of the devil? The snare of the devil is what snared him—pride. It is vital we comprehend that Jesus is good in us. Therefore, when we find ourselves lifted in pride, we will know we are closer to Satan and further from God.

Vine's Expository Dictionary of Old and New Testament Words translate the word good in 1st Timothy 3:7 as "*kalos*" which means *admirable, or becoming. Kalos* also has the ethical meaning of what is *fair, right, honorable, honest of such conduct as deserves esteem.*

Lucifer's conduct, what he made of himself, was the antithesis of good and God would not tolerate rebellion in heaven. Jesus said in Luke 10:18, *"I beheld Satan as lightning fall from heaven."* When we fail to allow Jesus to dwell in our hearts, we will find ourselves falling in life.

Fortunately, our falling does not have to be final or fatal. The Lord is able to keep us from falling (Jude 24), and this is possible when Jesus is on the inside of us working on the outside of us. However, if we happen to slip, because the Word of God informs us that good men do fall, the Lord holds us up with His hand.

> *"The steps of a good man are ordered by the Lord: and he delighteth in his way. Though he fall, he shall not be utterly cast down: for the Lord upholdeth him with his hand."* (Psalms 37:23-24)

When I ponder over the fact of God holding us in His hand, I can't help appreciating how God is good to us.

—Jesus Is Good to Us—

Adam and Eve fell in the garden because of disobedience. Like them, we too can fall and at some point, we all have. When we fall will God dismiss us as too bad to love? No! God's love is deep enough to reach those deemed untouchable and undeserving. God will do for us what He did for Adam and Eve. God helps us when we fall and cover us once we confess (Gen. 3:21). His love covers a multitude of sin (1st Pet. 4:8). God covers us because He's good to us.

God gave humanity all that was good. Why? Because, He gives us only what is good and not what is bad.

Some may ask, "What about the *tree of the knowledge of good and evil* (Gen. 2:9)? Why did God put that tree in the garden?" Many misread what God said. The tree was not evil; it was the tree of knowledge of good and evil. In the same garden, God put the *tree of life* (Gen. 2:9). Every day they were to eat from the tree of life. God had one prohibition: "Do not eat from the tree of the knowledge of good and evil (Gen. 2:17).

God withholds nothing that is profitable to us. If He instructs us not to do a particular thing, we better understand His instructions are for our good. What's so bad about the tree of knowledge of good and evil? Well, too much knowledge can puff us up (1st Cor. 8:1). Adam and Eve felt they knew what was good for their well-being.

Sometimes people can be too smart for their own good. You can have multiple degrees and think you know everything. Yet the degree tells you that you do not know everything. This is why it is called a degree... you only have a *degree, or portion of knowledge.*

Only God knows it all. Only God knows what is good for us. In Genesis 3:5, Satan says to Eve if you partake of the *knowledge of the tree of good and evil, you will become like God.* Any knowledge without God causes our ego to be inflated, or puffed up.

With a mindset such as this, we can find ourselves *independent* of God and *dependent* upon our will and knowledge. The Apostle Paul described people as those "*that did not like to retain God in their knowledge; God gave them over to a reprobate mind* (Rom. 1:28)."

God can no longer reach people that have made themselves independent of Him. God is good to us, but He can't give us of His abundance when we're in a state of disobedience. The problem with having the knowledge of good and evil is we become intimate with evil as much as we are with good.

The Bible says Eve saw the forbidden tree was *good* for food. This is how Satan was able to deceive her. Eve also saw the tree was good to make her wise. Therefore, the tree was desirable (*good*) for wisdom and armed with this knowledge, Eve underestimated God, which is *evil* (Gen. 3:6).

When you take the word *evil* and spell it backwards, it spells *live.* This is to say, evil is to live backwards or to live without God.

God is good to us. The Lord made us and is on the inside of us. Whoever believes they can live without God in any way is evil! I didn't say this kind of person is wicked, I said they are evil (living backwards). Love is a many splendored thing. God doesn't want anyone in this world trying to live without His love. God is good and the love He gives us is good.

Far too many are seeking the good life when they ought to be seeking the God-life. It is possible to have good without God, but it's impossible to have God without good. Knowing this can make the difference between merely a good life that can be removed at any time and a God-life that will always remain.

Here's a lesson all Christians need to know; Satan will never try a child of God with evil. The devil will present what appears good in order to pull us out of the will of God. Remember, *everything that is good is not God; but everything God is good.* The problem with good is it has one too many letter o's.

If asked which is better a book or a bike, what would be the answer? The proper answer is whichever is needed for the moment. The book is good to keep our minds sharp and the bike is good to keep us in shape. God is good to us. So, He gives us what's good as He determines what's needed at the time.

Everything God made was good. Nothing God made was evil. We obtain knowledge in two ways. Either we humble ourselves before God and let Him show us what is good, or we take it upon ourselves to acquire knowledge.

God knows us better than we know ourselves. Therefore, He knows everything we need. David said, "*I will praise thee; for I am fearfully and wonderfully made* (Psa. 139:14)." When God created us, He made us with different fingerprints and DNA. God did not copy anyone; He made everyone as an individual.

Jesus as the Good Shepherd, Great Shepherd and Chief Shepherd *knows and shows* His sheep what is good:

> *"He hath shewed thee, O man,* ***what is good****; and what doth the LORD require of thee, but to do justly, and to love mercy, and to walk humbly with thy God?"* (Micah 6:8 boldness added)

Love is a many splendored thing. God's love is so strong for us, He does not want us wandering and wondering what is good. When we yield our will in submission and obedience, God will show us what is good.

—Let's Be Good for Jesus—

Ponder the following passage carefully:

> *"I beseech you therefore, brethren, by the mercies of God, that ye present your bodies a living sacrifice, holy, acceptable unto God, which is your reasonable service. And be not conformed to this world: but be ye transformed by the renewing of your mind, that ye may prove what is that* ***good****, and acceptable, and perfect, will of God."* (Romans 12:1-2 boldness added)

The book of Romans is an interesting book to study. The crux of the first eleven chapters is about what Christ has done for His Church. Within the first eleven chapters we discover Jesus sanctifies, justifies, and redeems us. To put it plainly, Jesus is good to us.

Now, in the twelfth chapter the Apostle Paul conveys how we ought to behave.

> *"And be not conformed to this world: but be ye transformed by the renewing of your mind, that ye may prove what is that good, and acceptable, and perfect, will of God."* (Romans 12:2)

Paul says *be not* conformed to the world, because we have already *been* conformed to the world. The only way to break away from conformity is to be transformed by the renewing of our minds.

The word transformed is translated as "*metamorpho*"[31] or metamorphosis. It is like a caterpillar that transforms into a butterfly.

A caterpillar crawls on its belly and lives in the dirt. When it is time, the caterpillar goes through a metamorphosis and becomes a butterfly. Afterwards, the butterfly can never revert back to a caterpillar. In the butterfly state it flies everywhere, while as a caterpillar it was reduced to crawling.

In essence, Paul is saying, not to be conformed to this world, reduced to crawling, when we can fly high with the Lord. We ought to be what God has created us to be by the *renewing of our minds*. We do not *conform* when we are *transformed* because we are *informed.*

Paul also exhorts us: "*Prove what is that good, and acceptable, and perfect, will of God* (Rom. 12:2)." The word "prove" is the Greek word "*dokimazo.*" *Dokimazo* carries the connotation of *approve of something, by being tried and experienced, because of your practice and performance.*[32] God is not saying test it… God is saying prove it!

We prove God's will for us and our acceptance of His will with our love. All of us possess unique God given abilities. These abilities are what make us good. When we discover what our abilities are it is our responsibility not to squander them. Therefore, we must develop our abilities through the art of practice.

You can have a talent, but if you do not practice *it*, you will not be good at *it*. Some believe because they are naturally good at something they do not need to practice. Whatever the ability, it must be practiced or it will be wasted.

In the later portion of Philippians 4:18, Paul speaks of a

"*sacrifice acceptable, well pleasing to God.*" Paul is saying to the church at Philippi, that whatever we do, has to be pleasing to God. If we are not practicing what we are good at, how can it be beneficial it in its effect towards others? How do we make our abilities beneficial? We practice our abilities until they are acceptable and then they become perfect.

Perfect in the Bible does not mean flawless, unless, the subject of that perfection is God. The word perfect is *teleios* in Romans 12:2. Again, *teleios* means to *bring to full development, growth or maturity.*[33]

Goodness as love's character perfects us and enables us to love as God loves. In the context of loving our enemies Jesus says, "*Be ye therefore perfect even as your Father which is in heaven is perfect* (Matt. 5:48)." In other words, practice love until it's fully developed, grown or mature.

Someone may be born male, but that does not make him a man. As a male, he has to go through the process of manhood to reach full development, growth, and maturity. A male child is not a man at birth. The process is the same for a woman. The point is, we can be of a mature age and still not have gone through the process of becoming a good man or woman.

When we enter the military, the first requirement is to successfully complete basic training. In basic training, the drill sergeants' job parallels with Paul's admonition to his son in the faith Timothy. In 2nd Timothy 2:3 Paul says "*endure hardness as a good soldier.*" We can be soldiers, but not good ones.

The Drill Sergeant has the responsibility to *drill the process* of becoming a soldier into new recruits. He will make demands, and put as much pressure as possible on them. The Drill Sergeant knows that in the heat of the battle, a soldier will break down and give up if not trained to endure hardness.

The word hardness is translated as "*kakopatheo.*" This word means to *endure afflictions; not to be afraid of suffering for the Lord; to suffer hardships, troubles, problems, difficulties, and evils.*[34] If we are not able to handle the hardness, we will not be able to handle the war. We will quit in the midst of the fight.

We can be good for Jesus by enduring the hardness of life. In tough times we must allow God's love to prevail over the problems and pressures we face. The Holy Spirit, as our drill sergeant, prepares us for battle.

Life is not about flowery beds of ease or tiptoeing through the tulips. Life consists of bad things and even bad things happening to good people. Just remember, everything good doesn't come from God, but God brings everything that is good. Therefore, our mandate is to keep ourselves in the love of God. Love is a many splendored thing!

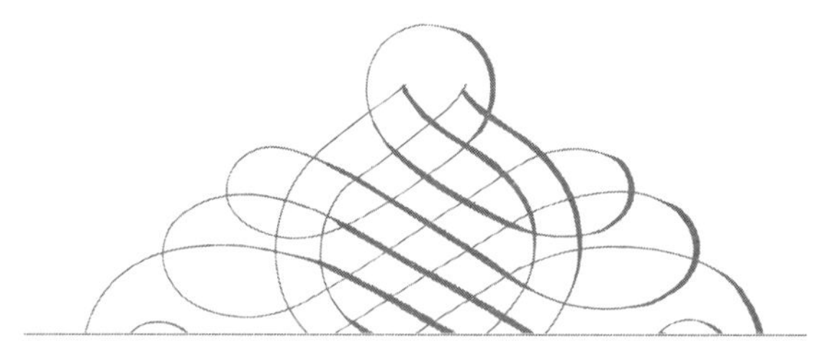

THE INGREDIENT OF LOVE

FAITHFULNESS

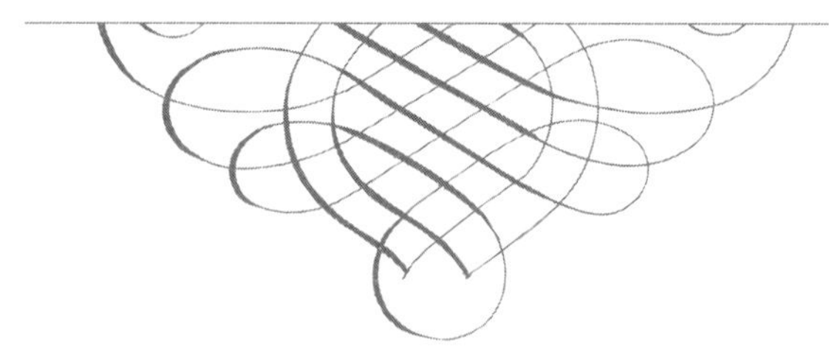

10

FAITHFULNESS IS LOVE'S LOYALTY

*"But the fruit of the spirit is love, joy, peace, long suffering, gentleness, goodness, **faith**..."*
(GALATIANS 5:22 BOLDNESS ADDED)

The Lord Jesus Christ has enabled us and counted us faithful, putting us into the ministry. The word "counted" carries the meaning "*to deem or esteem*."[35] The Lord esteems us and that is why He counts on us. This has caused me to understand the House of God is a ministry factory producing ministers.

> *"And I thank Christ Jesus our Lord, who hath enabled me, for that he counted me faithful, putting me into the ministry."* (1st Timothy 1:12)

The word *minister* in this passage is translated as *servant*. We love God and as a result of our love for Him, we serve Him. He counts us as faithful sons and daughters, enabling us to become fruitful. Make no mistake, fruitfulness results from faithfulness

(Matt. 25:21). And faithfulness is love's loyalty. Love is a many splendored thing.

—GOD CAN COUNT ON ME—

God is not into counting numbers. However, with God every number counts. This is simply to say God does not consider our strength in our numbers; our strength is counted by our loyalty to Him. Our significance is found in Him. We must learn to lean upon the Lord in every area of our lives. As we count on Him, He can count on us and only then are we considered faithful.

Love spawns faithfulness, which is the seventh manifestation of the fruit of the Spirit. Usually we do not start with being faithful to God; we start by attempting to be faithful to one another. This is a mistake. Trying to be faithful to others without the love of God could lead to disloyalty. However, when we generate our faithfulness toward God, His Spirit enables us to operate faithfully with others. If God can count on us then others can count on us.

Let's consider two Greek words that define *faith* and *faithfulness*. *Faith* is the Greek word "*pistis*" meaning *to trust and believe in.*[36] This is what Jesus was teaching in Mark 11:22 when He said, "Have faith in God." He was teaching us to trust and believe in God's promise and performance.

We find the concept of *faithful* in Galatians 5:22-23, and even though it says, "*faith,*" the Greek word is "*pistos,*" which means *faithful or faithfulness.* Faithfulness is different from just having trust or believing in someone. It carries the connotation of being dependable.

When we say God counted us "faithful," we are speaking of being dependable and reliable. Someone is considered reliable when they can be counted on first by God and then by others. This person possesses God's love and portrays a level of loyalty. Love is a many splendored thing!

The core of God's heart is that His people be found faithful. The basic ingredients of faithfulness (love's loyalty) are *integrity and fidelity.* These two ingredients are synonymous with honesty and faithfulness. When these two elements are combined, they equate "**truth.**"

One of my favorite allegories is that of Mr. Truth and Mr. Lie. One hot sunny day, Mr. Truth went down to the lake, took off all his clothes, and went for a swim. Mr. Lie came behind the Truth and saw his clothes unattended.

A malicious look came across Mr. Lie's face as he delightfully mused, "I've got an idea!" He then proceeded to take off his clothes and put on Truth's clothes. Soon after, Mr. Lie paraded around town in Mr. Truth's attire. He pretended to be the truth.

When Mr. Truth came out of the lake he discovered his clothes missing and Mr. Lie's clothes left in its place. Much to everyone's chagrin, Mr. Truth walked around town in the nude. When asked why he remained in the nude, Mr. Truth replied "*I would rather be known as the naked truth than to wear a lie.*"

We must endeavor to be truthful in every degree and in

every way. God's love empowers us to be truthful and faithful. To know the truth makes us free, and causes the Holy Spirit to help us. When we enter into a lie, the Holy Spirit retreats because He is the "*Spirit of truth*" (Jhn. 16:13).

We need God's Spirit in our lives to help us along the way. His Spirit reveals His love and receives our love for Him. Our love should convey our loyalty and declare we're on the Lord's side.

When we can love God according to the Shema of Israel, with all our heart, soul, mind, and strength, then we can love our neighbor as we love ourselves. At this point, we'll be truthful and faithful with our neighbors. Our faithfulness all stems from loving God first (Deut. 6:4-5/Matt. 22:37-40).

We love God because He first loved us (1st Jhn. 4:19). God loved us so much that He gave Jesus; Jesus' love compelled Him to lay down His life for us. Thus, He provided a way for us to avoid the terrors of hell, and inherit eternally life in Heaven. When it mattered most we could count on God; therefore, He should be able to count on us.

The simple fact is, if God cannot count on us, no one else can. There is no sense in counting on someone God cannot count on. If they are not faithful to Him, mark it down, sooner or later they will be unfaithful to others.

That's why it's so important to receive Jesus and appreciate His love. His love exudes His faithfulness which in turn is developed in our lives through virtuous disciplines. We must accept God's love then apply it through faithfulness.

—God Requires Faithfulness—

We are disqualified with God if we are not faithful. Without faith, it is impossible to please Him (Heb. 11:6). Faith is important, and faithfulness is important, too. God admires and requires people who are faithful.

God admires, desires, and requires faithfulness from us in every area of our lives. Likewise, we admire, desire, and require the same attribute in our relationships with others. Faithfulness is the result of a life of love. If a person loves what they do they will be faithful to do it. Without a doubt, if a person truly loves their spouse they will be faithful.

Many people have a charisma without substance. The Bible declares: "Faith is the substance… (Heb. 11:1)." People of faith exude faithfulness. The Lord doesn't require charisma, He gives us that. However, He does require us to be faithful. Gifts and talents are worthless without faithfulness.

Jesus said:

> *"He that is faithful in that which is least is faithful also in much: and he that is unjust in the least is unjust also in much."* (Luke 16:10)

The Amplified Version provides further insight into what Jesus was teaching His disciples:

> *"Therefore if you have not been faithful in the [case of] unrighteous mammon (deceitful riches, money, possessions), who will entrust to you the true riches? And if you have not*

> *proved faithful in that which belongs to another [whether God or man], who will give you that which is your own [that is, the true riches]? No servant is able to serve two masters; for either he will hate the one and love the other, or he will stand by and be devoted to the one and despise the other. You cannot serve God and mammon (riches, or anything in which you trust and on which you rely)."* (Luke 16:11-13)

Faithfulness is a quality of God's nature that cannot have divided loyalties. Again, without it we are unable to please God. Therefore, it stands to reason, He requires it.

The latter part of Romans 12:3 says God has given to every man the "*measure of faith*" or literally their portion of faith. The concept of the measure of faithfulness reminds me of this simple poem:

> *"I want to be able as the days go by, to look myself right in the eye; I don't want to stand with the setting of the sun, and hate myself for the things I have done."*—Edgar A. Guest

Consider the following passage:

> *"Let a man so account of us, as of the ministers of Christ, and stewards of the mysteries of God. Moreover, it is* ***required*** *in stewards, that a man be found faithful."*
> (1st Corinthians 4:1-2 boldness added)

A *steward* is someone who is entrusted with what belongs to someone else. We are stewards of God's grace. We are stewards of everything we have; nothing belongs to us by way of ownership. All that we possess is by way of our relationship with God.

Spiritually speaking, we cannot take any material possessions with us when we leave earth because we are only stewards. Because faithfulness is love's loyalty, it's not a request, but a requirement (Col. 3:23).

Faithfulness is a virtue we cannot buy. Those that are disloyal, like Judas, end up hanging themselves (Matt. 27:3-5). There is nothing more virtuous than being loyal to someone and letting that person know of our faithfulness. The Lord loves us undisputedly and He requires faithfulness in return. Therefore, it is encumbered upon us to comprehend the depth of faithfulness.

The Elements of Faithfulness

Any discussion of faithfulness and loyalty must include its essential elements—*integrity, fidelity* and *allegiance.* First, integrity is *an undivided and unbroken truth—truth no matter what.*

In the courtroom, a defendant or witness is asked to place their hand on the Bible. Then they are questioned, "Do you swear to tell the truth, the whole truth and nothing but the truth?" This is all based on integrity. Integrity involves telling the truth, the whole truth and nothing but the truth. A person who walks in integrity walks in wholeness and they are not a broken or divided person.

Second, there's the quality of fidelity. Fidelity is *the state or the quality of being faithful and truthful; it is the act of binding one's self to a particular course of action.*[37] Fidelity is rooted in the love of God. The Lord binds Himself to us. God said, "I'll never leave you, nor forsake you (Heb. 13:5)."

Another element of faithfulness is allegiance. Faithfulness is immersed in loyalty and loyalty translates into allegiance. When we were children, most of us recall reciting The Pledge of Allegiance:

"I pledge allegiance to the Flag of the United States of America, and to the Republic for which it stands, one Nation under God, indivisible, with liberty and justice for all."

The pledge of allegiance was an expression of loyalty to our federal flag and the republic of the United States. Moreover, it is to be an expression of our love for our country. It was adopted by Congress as the pledge in 1942.[38] The expression of God's loyalty is also demonstrated in this principle of *allegiance*. A principle is a fixed law of operation that leaves no room for negotiation, debate or discussion. The origin of this word allegiance can be traced back to the late 14th century from the Anglo-French word "*legaunce.*"[39]

In the 14th century, the word meant, "*loyalty of a liegeman (subject) to his lord or master.*" It's meaning has evolved to carry the connotation of devotion, and loyalty to a person or a cause. Our devotion for God should cause us to be faithful to Him.

We see an example of this truth as the reins of leadership passed from David to Solomon:

"The national leaders, the army officers, and his brothers all pledged their ***allegiance*** *to King Solomon."*
(1st Chronicles 29:24 LB boldness added)

In approximately 1400 B.C. Moses declared:

"You must worship no other gods, but only Jehovah, for he is

a God who claims absolute loyalty and exclusive devotion." (Exodus 34:14 LB)

Through love we offer God our allegiance, faithfulness and trust. Being faithful equates to being trusted. Trust is definitely an essential element of faithfulness.

Motivational speaker and best-selling author, Stephen Covey wrote a fantastic book years ago, *"The Speed of Trust."* It deals with character and the concept of trust. In it, he gives the correlation between trust, speed and cost. He points out when trust is *low*, speed is *slow* and cost is *high*. Conversely, when trust is *high*, speed is *high* and cost is *low*.

An example of this principle is seen in our modern airports. Passengers have to check-in to the airport an hour earlier than their flight is scheduled to depart. Passengers must arrive earlier to clear security check points. In this case, trust in the passengers is low, the time it takes to get to the plane is slower and the cost it takes to fly has risen in order to provide security check points and the like.

When trust is low in any relationship, that relationship is a bad one. This holds especially true with the relationship between a pastor and the parishioners. This is why God requires His ministers to be faithful when they are preaching His Word. If the people don't trust the one preaching the Word, it could hinder the Word and God's love from reaching the people with the power to change their lives.

There's nothing more awful than a preacher who cannot be

trusted. It's like having a beautiful gown on display in a department store window and a child smears the glass with chocolate. Now, when people come to view the gown on display they are unable to appreciate it.

The gown is not smeared, it is still beautiful, but the window is dirty. When a preacher is dishonest he smears the display of God's love through His Son Jesus. Love is a many splendored thing. Therefore, when we love God we'll display it through the element of truthfulness.

One of the most profound examples of trust is seen in the relationship of Jonathan and his armor bearer:

> *"And Jonathan said to the young man that bare his armor, Come, and let us go over unto the garrison of these uncircumcised: it may be that the LORD will work for us: For there is no restraint to the LORD to save by many or by few. And his armor bearer said unto him, Do all that is in thine heart: turn thee; behold, I am with thee according to thy heart.* (1st Samuel 14:6-7)

The original Hebrew for this word heart is "*le-bab.*"[40] It means an inner reflection of the outer man. It further means the "*totality of a person's nature and character.*" The character of Jonathan's armor bearer was full of faithfulness (love's loyalty). You cannot have authentic loyalty without love (agape) and you cannot have authentic love (agape) without loyalty.

Jonathan's trust and faithfulness to God compelled him to move forward against what appeared to be an overwhelming enemy force. Although greatly outnumbered by the Philistines, Jonathan trusted God and his armor bearer trusted him.

Love is a many splendored thing. This catalyst of love created a chain reaction of faith that was released among God's people (See verses 16-22).

The victory God gave His people through Jonathan and his armor bearer, is the same God desires to give us. We can claim it through love's loyalty—faithfulness.

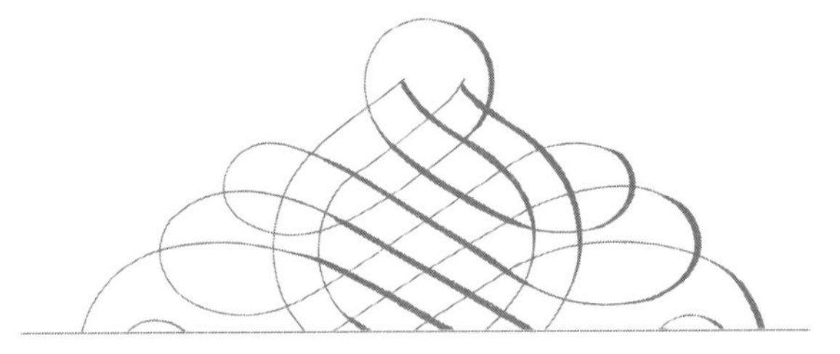

THE INGREDIENT OF LOVE

MEEKNESS

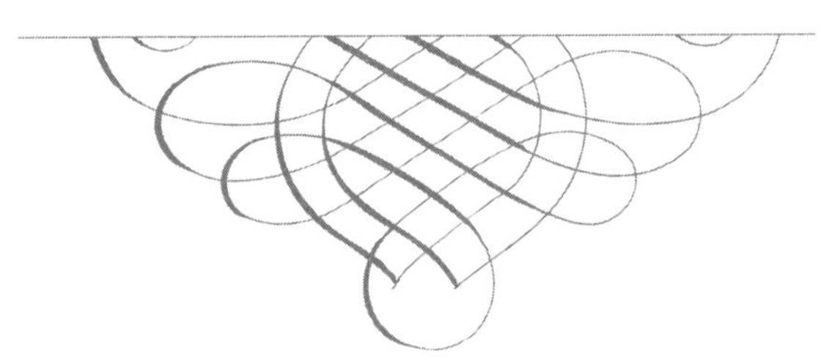

11

MEEKNESS IS LOVE'S HUMILITY

"But the fruit of the spirit is love, joy, peace, long suffering, gentleness, goodness, faith, ***meekness...****"*

(GALATIANS 5:22-23 BOLDNESS ADDED)

The fruit of the spirit is love and through love the character of Christ is developed within us. When Jesus is developed in us, love is expressed in a powerful and profuse manner.

In Galatians 5:23, we find the word meekness. This is the eighth virtue of the fruit of the Spirit. Meekness is love's humility. The word meekness in this text is "*praus;*" which means having "*controlled power under divine authority.*"[41] Meekness is what keeps us from being out of control.

—Being Under God's Control—

The Bible tells us in 1st Peter 5:5, we are to be "clothed with humility." The word humility in this passage is the Greek word "*tapeinos*." *Tapeinos* carries the meaning of always being under divine authority.[42] Meekness and humility are interchangeable. They're as close as wet is to water. You cannot have one without the other. Just as the wet cannot be separated from water; meekness and humility share the same paradigm, they are inseparable.

Jesus was recorded saying:

> "*Come unto me, all ye that labour and are heavy laden, and I will give you rest. Take my yoke upon you, and learn of me; for I am* ***meek*** *and* ***lowly*** *in heart: and ye shall find rest unto your souls.*" (Matthew 11:28-29 boldness added)

The word lowly in this passage is the same Greek word as humble or humility (*tapeinos*). To have a meek and lowly spirit takes maturity. Jesus, who is the very expression of God's love, placed before us a pattern to follow. For our benefit, He was not intimidated or ashamed to become lowly and meek. The level of a person's maturity is their ability to yield their will in submission and obedience with humbleness and meekness.

Our maturity is measured by our willingness to submit to God. This is not a difficult task when we understand how much God loves us. Love is a many splendored thing and we get to enjoy it when we allow the Lord to control our lives. Through His love He guides and guards us.

An excellent metaphor for meekness is that of a horse under the control of a rider. The rider controls the horse, yet the spirit of the horse is not broken. The horse continues to gallop and stride.

By all means, the horse retains its stamina and strength. In fact, the horse still has power but it is under the control of the rider.

The rider and horse analogy should depict the control Jesus has in our lives. This is possible only through our love for God. When we know God loves us and we place our trust in His love, we'll release the power of our ambitions and attitudes to Him.

The following passage admonishes us:

> *"I will instruct thee and teach thee in the way which thou shalt go: I will guide thee with mine eye. Be ye not as the horse, or as the mule, which have no understanding: whose mouth must be held in with bit and bridle, lest they come near unto thee."* (Psalms 32:8-9)

Our soul consists of the mind, emotions, and will. God has given us a free will to choose our path or direction in life. Therefore, the *real* power is the *will* power. It is what we will to do and what we will not do that makes the difference between receiving victory with God or not.

In the garden of Gethsemane Jesus said, "*not as I will but thy will be done*" (Lu. 22:42). In every given situation, every decision we make should come under God's will. This is easy to do when we understand the genuine love He has for us. Meekness is not weakness; it's our willingness to allow God to take control.

—Understanding Submission—

Understanding is critical if we are to obtain and maintain God's blessings in our lives.

Consider the following passages:

"Trust in the Lord with all your heart and lean not to your own understanding." (Proverbs 3:5)

"Wisdom is the principle thing; therefore get wisdom: and with all thy getting get understanding." (Proverbs 4:7)

Think about it, when we get a car, we must get an understanding of how the car operates. Having keys to the car is not enough. We must possess a basic understanding of the car's function in order to enjoy its amenities.

When couples marry and say, "I do," eventually they will discover what they "did." It is vital that they get an understanding of marriage, because if they fail to, they will end up with a shattered and broken relationship.

From this premise, it is essential that we get an understanding of meekness—loves humility. Only by this understanding are we able to submit through meekness and receive God's grace in return.

"Likewise, ye younger, submit yourselves unto the elder. Yea, all of you *be subject one to another, and be clothed with humility: for God resisteth the proud, and giveth grace to the humble."* (1st Peter 5:5)

Vine's Expository Dictionary of Old and New Testament Words translates the words *submit* and *subject* with the same Greek word "*hupotasso.*" Hupotasso means to *rank under; obey; to be subject to.*

The Scripture records:

> "*Humble yourselves therefore under the mighty hand of God, that he may exalt you in due time.*" (1st Peter 5:6)

Understand, God will never humble us; this is something we must do for ourselves. Although He will not humble us, He will humiliate us. Therefore, it's best to humble ourselves by keeping ourselves in the love of God (Jude 21). God instructs us to humble ourselves *under* His mighty hand. We cannot expect God's hand to be over our family, finances, future, etc. if we are not willing to get under His hand of instruction, correction and direction.

When we are willing to submit to God's love and leading, He will bless us with what is good. Jesus remarked, "*Blessed are the meek: for they shall inherit the earth* (Matt. 5:5)." Many have not received their inheritance simply because there is no meekness or submission.

God is not opposed to our succeeding in life. He said to Joshua:

> "*This book of the law shall not depart out of thy mouth; but thou shalt meditate therein day and night, that thou mayest observe to do according to all that is written therein: for then thou shalt make thy way prosperous, and then thou shalt have **good success.***" (Joshua 1:8 boldness added)

Our good success which is God's success depends solely on loving God to such a degree that we meditate on His Word day and night. When we love Him reading His Word is not viewed as a chore, but a chance to know Him more. His Word is His love letter to us. It reveals His heart toward us and reels our hearts towards Him.

Submission displays our love for the Lord. It protects us from the adversary. The Apostle James admonishes us:

> *"Submit yourselves therefore to God. Resist the devil, and he will flee from you."* (James 4:7)

It does no good to resist the devil without first submitting to God. The devil can take what belongs to us, but he cannot take what belongs to God. Therefore, it becomes imperative that we submit all we have and who we are to the Lord. Now, everything we have and who we are is off limits to the devil.

Realize it is the devil's plot, ploy and plan to trip us up. And pride is the core of that plan. It is the Achilles tendon of submission. However, love is God's way of combating pride. The Apostle Paul wisely advises, "Not to think of yourself more highly than you ought to think but to think soberly… (Rom. 12:3)." In other words, God wants us to sober up. Vine's Expository Dictionary of Old and New Testament Words define soberness as "*temperate, self-controlled and discreet.*" God is not saying we should not think highly of our self, He conveys, *do not think more highly!*

The submissive and meek attitude always accepts God's will because "Father knows best." A humble attitude is one of gratitude. Meekness causes us not to walk around pouting, or doubting God's will for us. We become grateful for His love and the authority He set in place.

—Submission Gives Us Authority—

There is a revelation of a difference between power (ability) and power (authority). We discussed earlier in this chapter, *the level of a man's maturity is the ability to yield his will in submission and obedience.* This is having controlled power. That word power is ability. In other words, we have controlled ability. In this sense, ability and power are synonymous.

> *"Behold, I give unto you power to tread on serpents and scorpions, and over all the power of the enemy: and nothing shall by any means hurt you."* (Luke 10:19)

The word *behold* carries the meaning of insight beyond sight. Jesus used the word behold, He was seeking to give us the revelation of a difference in His usage of the word "power." Jesus says, "*Behold, I give unto you **power** to tread on serpents and scorpions, and over all the **power** of the enemy...*" A clearer and more concise translation of Jesus' declaration is He gives us "*power over the power of the devil.*"

The first usage of the word power is *exousia. Exousia* is authority. Vine's Expository Dictionary of Old and New Testament Words says that *exousia* means *the right to act, used of God, it is absolute and unrestricted.* The second usage of the word power in the text carries the meaning of ability. In its original Greek etymology, the word power is translated as *dunamis,* where our English word dynamite derives. Vine's says that *dunamis* also carries the meaning *of power—physical or moral ability as residing in a person or thing.*

Love is a many splendored thing! Through His love He grants us authority (*exousia*) over all the ability (*dunamis*) of Satan. He wants to empower us because He loves us. It is not *ability* that we need; rather *authority*. And this authority is given through the Father's love.

Metaphorically, it is like a police officer directing traffic. When the officer throws up a hand to stop or direct traffic, no words have to be spoken. The officer simply utilizes sign language. Now, the driver of the car possesses the ability to run over the officer. However, the driver stops because of the authority the officer possesses.

God has given us His love and approval and that's all the authority we need. God's authorization means He has moved on our behalf. We just need to humble ourselves under God's mighty hand; therefore, all authority in heaven and earth is behind us.

Now, what qualifies us to operate in God's authority is our capacity to serve under authority. In 1st Peter 5:5, the word subject and submit have the same meaning. The word subject is the Greek word "*hupotasso*." *Hupo* means under; *tasso* is arrangement and it's a military term that means *to rank under*.

There is equality in creation but priority in authority. For instance, there are women who are over men in the military because of their rank. If you are a soldier, it makes no difference whether your leader is male or female. The leadership structure is determined by a ranking system. This is what Paul stated: "*Let every soul be subject unto the higher powers. For there is no power but of God: the powers that be are ordained of God* (Rom. 13:1)."

Whoever is in authority has a responsibility to God. Authority always comes with responsibility.

—Meekness Submits To Authority—

We must be quick to love and serve others with the same love God expresses to us. His love empowers us with His authority to make a significant change in the lives of others. However, when we are not under God's authority, our responsibility is hindered and hampered.

Resistance to God's authority opens the door for demonic vexation and oppression. Someone may retort, "I'm saved!" Yes, but the question is have you submitted yourself to Jesus' Lordship? Jesus stated: *"And why call ye me, Lord, Lord, and do not the things which I say* (Lu. 6:46)*?"*

Immediately following this question, Jesus tells a parable:

> *"Whosoever cometh to me, and heareth my sayings, and doeth them, I will show you to whom he is like: He is like a man which built an house, and digged deep, and laid the foundation on a rock: and when the flood arose, the stream beat vehemently upon that house, and could not shake it: for it was founded upon a rock. But he that heareth, and doeth not, is like a man that without a foundation built an house upon the earth; against which the stream did beat vehemently, and immediately it fell; and the ruin of that house was great."* (Luke 6: 47-49)

In the previous parable, both houses were built, but one fell and one did not. How did this occur? Simple, one house fell because the man was not submitted unto Jesus.

We previously read where Paul said, "*Let every soul be subject unto the higher authority*" and it begins with spiritual authority. God's love does not restrict, it protects. The Lord knows there's safety in submitting to authority. The first authority is always spiritual authority.

The question becomes, "Who is our pastor?" It does not matter which church we may attend. Being subject to higher spiritual authority pragmatically means, we need a pastor. We cannot be committed to God if we are not connected with our spiritual leader. To be disconnected from our pastor is to be disconnected from the will of God which is to "*be subject to the higher authority.*"

God's love for us compels Him to give us spiritual leaders who will feed and reveal His purpose and plan. Make no mistake; accepting our pastors is like receiving the heart of the Father. The Scripture reveals: "*And I will give you pastors according to mine heart, which shall feed you with knowledge and understanding* (Jer. 3:15)."

The Bible gives us a pattern by which to further understand the precept of submission to authority that intersects with meekness as love's humility.

> *"But I would have you know, that the head of every man is Christ; and the head of the woman is the man; and the head of Christ is God."* (1st Corinthians 11:3)

The previous passage is not speaking on equality; but rather priority. The apostolic pattern deems that one must be first; someone second, and another if necessary, third, if there is to be order in the house.

The pattern set forth in 1st Corinthians 11:3 began with spiritual authority, which is God, Christ, spiritual headship (male or female) based upon the person's salvation and relationship with God. Spiritual authority moves into domestic authority. The order in domestic authority is God, Christ, husband (saved or unsaved), wife and after that children. Then we move into public authority—God, Christ, president, vice president, etc.

Of the three realms described, there is desperate need for meekness in the domestic arena. So, the same can be said of God's love. When we truly have the love of God operating from our hearts, it will manifest in the way we treat one another in the home.

In the domestic realm, the man is to be *ahead* of the woman. The man is not *the* head he is to be *ahead*. When couples marry, they do so side by side, this indicates equality. Nevertheless, the man is to take the first position in the domestic ranking, this indicates priority.

Therefore, the husband is called the house-band man. The house-band man keeps the house banded together. When I was younger, I can recall when solicitors came to our door, they would ask, "Is the man of the house home?" This is not to diminish the status of the wife, it only provided her with proper covering.

There is nothing more attractive than a woman who submits herself to her husband. This sign of meekness is not weakness, rather it's her strength being revealed through her willingness to love and obey. This causes a real man to humble himself and seek the heart and direction of God.

The first order of business for the husband is to lead his family in prayer. Prayer produces intimacy. We become intimate with the One we pray to (God); the one we pray with (spouse); the ones we pray for (children, family, friends, etc.). If the husband is out of place, the wife is displaced, and the children are misplaced. Because of love, we cover each other in prayer. Love is a many splendored thing!

Jesus meekly submitted to God and increase was the result.

> *"And he went down with them, and came to Nazareth,* ***and was subject unto them****: but his mother kept all these sayings in her heart. And* ***Jesus increased*** *in wisdom and stature, and in favour with God and man."* (Luke 2:51-52 boldness added)

Jesus was rewarded with increase first with God and then with others He encountered, because He submitted to His earthly parents. However, He didn't stop there! Jesus also submitted to spiritual authority.

> *"Then cometh Jesus from Galilee to Jordan unto John, to be baptized of him. But John forbad him, saying, I have need to be baptized of thee, and comest thou to me?"* (Matthew 3:13-14)

Jesus submitted himself unto the spiritual authority of John. He didn't say, "I'm calling the shots!" No, Jesus submitted Himself to God's will and more importantly, God's way. He was able to submit because of God's love.

God's love is made perfect in our submission. Don't miss God's blessing because of pride. We must allow meekness—love's humility, to elevate us to a place where we may increase with God and man.

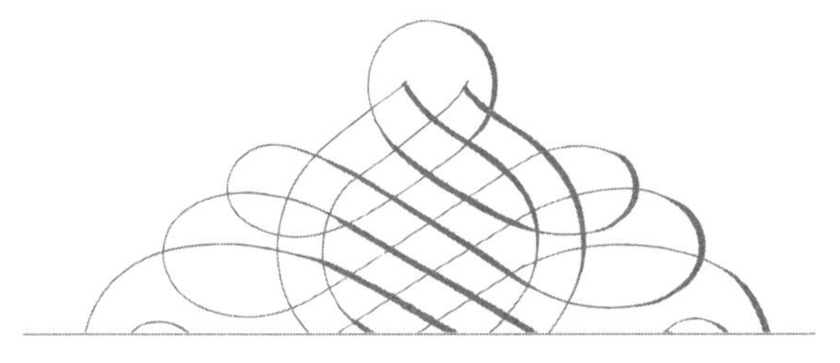

THE INGREDIENT OF LOVE
TEMPERANCE

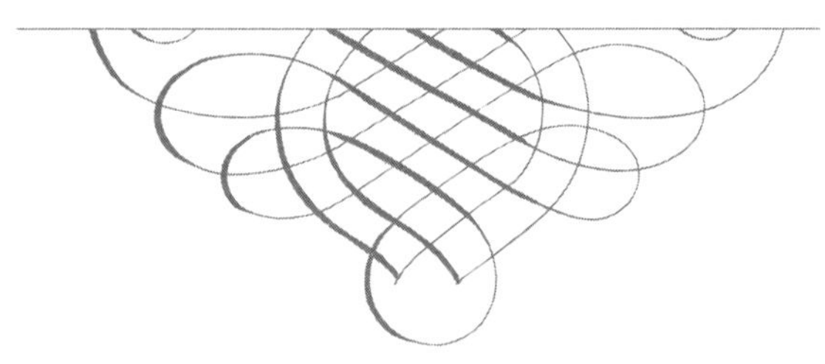

12

TEMPERANCE IS LOVE'S VICTORY

"But the fruit of the spirit is love, joy, peace, long suffering, gentleness, goodness, faith, meekness, ***temperance****: against such there is no law."*

(GALATIANS 5:22-23 BOLDNESS ADDED)

Let's recap the manifestations of the fruit of the Spirit. First of all, *love* is the fruit our Lord is looking to develop in us. *Joy* is love's strength, *peace* is love's safety, *longsuffering* is love's patience, *gentleness* is love's conduct, *goodness* is love's character, *faithfulness* is love's loyalty, *meekness* is love's humility, and now we come to ***temperance*** which is love's victory. This aggregate of virtues expresses God's love; however, temperance is the regulating virtue.

The English transliteration of the word temperance is "*enkrateia*." *Enkrateia* carries the meaning of *self-control, to master and control the body or the sinful nature with all of its desires and lusts.*[43] Temperance is what regulates the other fruit of the Spirit, so if we do not have temperance, the other fruit of the spirit will not operate productively.

—KEEP IT TOGETHER—

Anybody can be happy when things are happening the way they want them to happen. If we are not happy when things are going our way, something is definitely wrong with us. However, when things are *not* going our way, what do we do? Is this a time to fall apart? Certainly not! When things go awry we need temperance to help us keep it together.

If temperance is not operating in our lives we will have temper tantrums. It does not matter a person's age, temper tantrums may appear at moments of distress if there is a lack of temperance. Without temperance, self is simply out of control. A dearth of temperance leaves a person void of victory.

Temperance is love's victory and love is a many splendored thing. Victory for a Christian is internal before it's external.

> ***"And to know the love of Christ,*** *which passeth knowledge, that ye might be filled with all the fullness of God."* (Ephesians 3:19 boldness added)

Knowing the love of God internally fills us with all the fullness of God. God is love (1st Jhn. 4:8). To "know" in the previous passage means to be aware of, feel, possess, perceive, be resolved, or understand.

To know the love of God is to possess the power and presence of God's love. This enables us to face opposing circumstances and not lose our composure. We are able to keep it together when we can stop in the name of love. Temperance allows us to keep ourselves in the love of God and not fall to pieces when it seems everything around us is falling apart.

Tragically, many cannot stop in the name of love because they do not know or operate in the love of God. Consequently, they cannot control themselves. Spiritually speaking, temperance carries the connotation of strength and self-control. Further defined, temperance is love's victory through the *principle of Lordship* and *obedience to His Lordship*. If we are going to experience God's success, we have to control ourselves in any situation. We have to keep it together if we are going to live victoriously.

—Temperance Brings Victory—

> *"But thanks be to God, which giveth us the victory through our Lord Jesus Christ."* (1st Corinthians 15:57)

The Greek word for victory is "*nike*."[44] The word victory means to conquer or overcome. It is God's desire for us to overcome, conquer, and win.

Victory is not something we achieve as a goal, it's something we receive as a gift; because of whom we believe to be our God. The Bible records: "*But we are not of them that draw back unto prediction; but of them that believe to the saving of the soul* (Heb. 10:39)."

If our souls are not saved then we never overcome. I use the terms "overcome" and "victory" synonymously. Many people think victory is obtained through accomplishments and achievements.

This is not true. Temperance gives us the power to control ourselves, thus making us overcomers.

Temperance is love's victory through the principle of Lordship. The principle of Lordship recognizes that Jesus is Lord over our lives. There is nowhere in the Bible that suggests Jesus is to be our Savior and never our Lord. Knowing and applying this principle to my own life has helped me tremendously.

I remember when I came around a crucial corner with God. In other words, I had an epiphany that brought me to another level of maturity with Him. I learned a principle which is a divine law. It is a fixed principle of operation and it leaves no room for negotiation, debate, or discussion. The Lord taught me this principle of Lordship: If there is an area in our lives over which Jesus is not Lord and we refuse to allow Him to be Lord, we will find ourselves falling and failing in other areas where we once had victory. This is called backsliding.

The way of the Christian life is progression, it is always forward. To slide back is to *regress* and not *progress*. Temperance—love's victory makes it possible to overcome those things that keep us from moving forward, and provides us with the discipline to follow our Lord, completely.

> *"Only be thou strong and very courageous, that thou mayest* ***observe to do*** *according to all the law, which Moses my servant commanded thee: turn not from it to the right hand or to the left, that thou mayest prosper whithersoever thou goest."* (Joshua 1:7 boldness added)

Joshua and the people of God prospered and progressed because of their obedience to the Word of the Lord. However, it is imperative to understand we cannot progress if there is an area of our lives we have not allowed Jesus to have supremacy.

If Jesus is Lord, He chooses the way, clears the way and confirms the way as He did for Joshua. If temperance is not operating in our lives, it's because we have not made Jesus Lord. The Christian's victory comes only through submitting to Jesus' Lordship and receiving His love.

> *"Nay, in all these things we are more than conquerors through him that loved us."* (Romans 8:37)

However, when we distrust Jesus or deny Him complete authority, we come short of receiving His victory. If Jesus is Lord, our response is always an emphatic "Yes!" We can say, "No," but we can never say, "No Lord." The minute we say no is the moment we reveal He is not our Lord. When Jesus is not our Lord our final experience is one of defeat not victory. There is no halfway house with God! Jesus is to be Lord in all, through all, of all, or not at all!

This has nothing to do with the salvation of one's soul; however, it opens the door to disappointment, distress, and defeat. Love is a many splendored thing and God's love brings us victory.

> *"But thanks be unto God, which giveth us the victory through our Lord Jesus Christ."* (1st Corinthians 15:57)

In the original Greek our English word "Lord" is translated as "*kurios*." *Kurios* carries the meaning of *supreme in authority; Master; Owner. One to who service is due.*[45]

Some may ask, "Why am I going through such trauma and drama in life?" Others may ponder why they lack joy and fulfillment in life. The question becomes, "Is Jesus Lord of your life?"

Concerning obedience and Lordship Jesus says: *"Why call ye me, Lord, Lord, and do not the things which I say* (Lu. 6:46)*?"* The same verse in the Message Bible records: "*Why are you so polite with me, always saying 'Yes, sir,' and 'That's right, sir,' but never doing a thing I tell you*?

Unquestionably, we need to allow Jesus lordship in our lives. He knows us better than we know ourselves. His love for us is unbelievable. His desire is to bring us victory, but we must follow Him. This takes temperance and obedience.

—TEMPERANCE: JUST DO IT—

> "*These words I speak to you are not mere additions to your life, homeowner improvements to your standard of living. They are foundation words, words to build a life on. If you work the words into your life, you are like a smart carpenter who dug deep and laid the foundation of his house on bedrock. When the river burst its banks and crashed against the house, nothing could shake it; it was built to last. But if you just use my words in Bible studies and don't work them into your life, you are like a dumb carpenter who built a house but skipped the foundation. When the swollen river came crashing in, it collapsed like a house of cards. It was a total loss.*"
> (Luke 6: 47-49 MSG)

Jesus was a carpenter by profession. To build well, you must know how to build and what to build upon. This includes hearing and following instructions. Obedience to Jesus' Lordship entails learning to "*just do it.*"

> *"And the third day there was a marriage in Cana of Galilee; and the mother of Jesus was there: And both Jesus was called, and his disciples, to the marriage. And when they wanted wine, the mother of Jesus saith unto him, They have no wine. Jesus saith unto her, Woman, what have I to do with thee? Mine hour is not yet come. His mother saith unto the servants, Whatsoever he saith unto you, do it."* (John 2:1-5)

Mary, the mother of Jesus says to the servants, "Whatever He (Jesus) says, just do it." Temperance—love's victory is bringing ourselves under control and it is obedience to His Lordship. Just do it!

Vine's Expository Dictionary of Old and New Testament Words translate our English word *do* in John 2:5 as "*poieo*" in the original Greek. *Poieo* carries the connotation to "*form a routine or a habit of doing something.*" It is in the practicing of a thing that perfection takes place.

Through temperance we learn to form habits. We don't always want to do the things we have to do like going to work or school. Even still, we learn to just do it. The concept, "just do it" involves forming habits. In its original Latin root, the word habit addresses both "*the inner and outer states of being. It also means a customary practice, to have, to hold, or to possess.*"[46]

When we possess a love for Jesus, worship becomes a customary practice that perfects the performance of our attitude of gratitude *in* worship. It is not through coercion or compulsion that we form a habit of worship. It is out of adoration, and an attitude of gratitude that *we get* to worship Him because Jesus is Lord!

Temperance—love's victory brings us under the principle and obedience to His Lordship that forms *a habit* of obedience in us! The very foundation of our obedience should be to please God.

What pleases God is obedience. Through our obedience we become good hearers and doers of the Word.

God says to Joshua:

> "*This book of the law shall not depart out of thy mouth; but thou shalt meditate therein day and night that thou mayest* ***observe to do...***" (Joshua 1:8 boldness added)

Temperance causes the child of God to tackle any obstacle with the mantra, "Just do it!" By this mantra we learn to obey the voice of our Lord. Obedience to His Lordship forms *a habit* that trains the Believer in the art of *routinizing*. The term routinizing means to do something repeatedly until we become good at it. Once we're good at something we'll experience victory in that area.

Repetition gives us the ability to become good at what we do. To become good at obeying God opens the door to success in every area of our lives. The habit of routinizing enables a husband to become a good husband; it develops a parent into a good parent. Whatever we are we become good at it if we understand the art of routinizing.

In other words, just keep doing it! We must keep doing what we are doing to make a habit of it, to make it become a part of our lives.

Temperance and the art of routinizing are cut from the same cloth—discipline. Because of discipline we are able to keep ourselves in the love of God (Jude 21). And, God's love for us compels Him to give us victory.

> *"By this we come to know (recognize and understand) that we love the children of God: when we love God and* ***obey His commands*** *(orders, charges)—[when we keep His ordinances and are mindful of His precepts and His teaching]. For the [true] love of God is this: that* ***we do His commands*** *[keep His ordinances and are mindful of His precepts and teaching]. And these orders of His are not irksome (burdensome, oppressive, or grievous). For whatever is born of God is* ***victorious*** *over the world; and this is the* ***victory*** *that conquers the world, even our faith."* (1st John 5:2-4 boldness added AMP)

Listen, when it comes to temperance, we don't *have to do it*, but by God's grace, we *get to do it*. Before long, we *love to do it.* Through the principle of His Lordship and obedience to His Lordship, God has given us victory that overcomes the world. Temperance is love's victory!

THE PROOF OF LOVE
MERCY

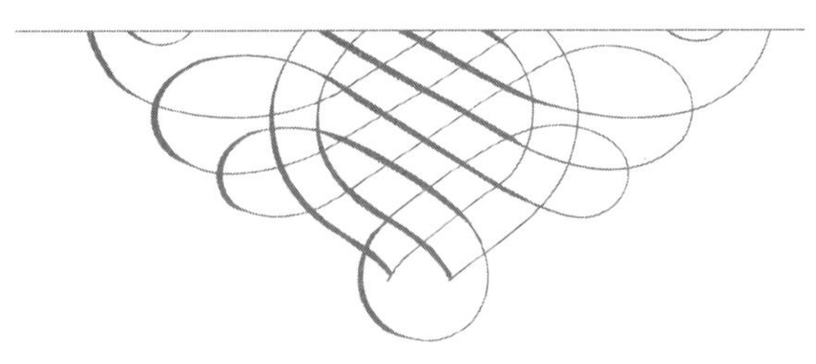

13

MERCY THE PROOF OF LOVE

"It is of the LORD'S mercies that we are not consumed, because his compassions fail not."

(LAMENTATIONS 3:22)

The greatest place to find ourselves is in the love of God. In His love are all the essentials to live a successful life. God's Spirit reveals His love and leads us to people whereby we share His love. Now, here lies the test of love. Apart from Jesus, all have come short of the mark. We all have offended someone at some point and we all have been offended. When we are offended, when someone disappoints us, what should be our response? The proper response to the test of offense should be to extend mercy.

Mercy is the proof of love. 1st John 4:8,16 divulges God is love, but He is also a merciful God. Mercy is the proof of God's love and He wants to reflect His love in and through us. This can happen when we accept His life and are cognizant of His lordship.

—We Find Mercy in Jesus' Lordship—

"Keep yourselves in the love of God, ***looking for the mercy of our Lord Jesus Christ*** *unto eternal life."*
(Jude 1:21 boldness added)

As Christians it is vital we look for the mercy of our Lord Jesus Christ. This is to say, we never forget His love and mercy toward us and we stay ready to extend that same love and mercy toward others. This is easier to do when we remember Jesus Christ is Lord.

We are saved by receiving Jesus Christ as Savior but oftentimes we fail to allow Him to be the Lord of our lives. If He is Lord, then it is never, "No Lord," it is always "Yes Lord." Jesus asked the following question: *"And why call ye me, Lord, Lord, and do not the things which I say* (Lu. 6:46)*?"* What the Lord says concerning our lives is what brings success in our lives.

Love is a many splendored thing. Those who have love are truly free from this world's downward spiral. This world has a way of trying to bring us down to its level. However, God has called us to a higher elevation. That elevation is to love and not hate. The proof of living above the everyday common fray of this world's negativity and hypocrisy is our ability to extend mercy.

Jonah had to learn mercy in a most unusual way.

"Now the word of the LORD came unto Jonah the son of Amittai, saying, Arise, go to Nineveh, that great city, and cry against it; for their wickedness is come up before me." (Jonah 1:1-2)

God commanded Jonah to deliver His Word to the wicked nation of Nineveh. Jonah knew that God was a merciful God. He understood if the Ninevites repented, God would not bring judgment upon them. Albeit, Jonah was a prejudicial preacher and he wanted God to smite and destroy Nineveh. Therefore, he ran from the presence of the Lord. Consequently, he went down to Tarshish, and paid his own fare.

> *"But Jonah rose up to flee unto Tarshish from the presence of the LORD, and went down to Joppa; and he found a ship going to Tarshish: so he paid the fare thereof, and went down into it, to go with them unto Tarshish from the presence of the LORD."* (Jonah 1:3)

Jesus' Lordship must be first and foremost if mercy is to go forth. We can't fail to crown Him as Lord, yet expect Him to promote us through life. Whenever we go our own way, we pay our own way. If we ask someone to lunch we should be ready to take up the tab; if someone invites us it should be the opposite. Wherever God sends us, He's accountable for all expenses and He delights in providing for us. His love for us compels Him to provide for us. However, when we refuse to go His way, His love allows us that latitude.

It was Jonah who decided to leave God's presence not the other way around. God will never leave us nor forsake us; He is faithful (Heb. 13:5). Regardless of the trouble we are in, as children of God He will always be there. However, if we go somewhere that we should not go, we must pay our own fare.

Jesus must be Lord of all or not at all. The purpose of His Lordship is for us to be a sign unto the Ninevites, which is a sign unto the world. When Jesus is Lord of our lives we can show the world what God is like; that God is love. The mercy of God upon Jonah's life is what caused the wicked city of Nineveh to turn around. Moreover, the mercy of God upon our lives gives others the same opportunity.

—We Find Mercy in— Jesus' Chastening

"Blessed are the merciful: for they shall obtain mercy." (Matthew 5:7)

God is a merciful God. As a matter of fact, the top of the Ark of the Covenant of God was called the mercy seat. This symbolized the throne from which God ruled Israel.

Jesus being merciful died for humanity's sin. His crucifixion on the cross has paid our ultimate fare—death, and prevented possible eternal separation from God. For that, He reserves the right to chastise us when we are out of the will of God. His chastisement is not a reflection of loathing; rather it's a result of His love.

The follow passage points to this:

"And ye have forgotten the exhortation which speaketh unto you as unto children, My son, despise not thou the ***chastening*** *of the Lord, nor faint when thou art rebuked of him: For whom*

> *the Lord loveth he* ***chasteneth****, and scourgeth every son whom he receiveth. If ye endure* ***chastening****, God dealeth with you as with sons; for what son is he whom the father* ***chasteneth*** *not?"* (Hebrews 12:5-7 boldness added)

Earlier we discovered Jonah's disobedience to God's assignment of mercy. Then we witnessed God's mercy on display as he chastened Jonah.

> *"But the LORD sent out a great wind into the sea, and there was a mighty tempest in the sea, so that the ship was like to be broken...And they said every one to his fellow, Come, and let us cast lots, that we may know for whose cause this evil is upon us. So they cast lots, and the lot fell upon Jonah...Then were the men exceedingly afraid, and said unto him, Why hast thou done this? For the men knew that he fled from the presence of the LORD, because he had told them."* (Jonah 1:4, 7,10)

The preceding scriptures reveal the chastening of God. Jonah didn't blame the devil for his misfortune. He knew it was God's hand bringing the punishment. Jonah was stubborn without mercy and he was prepared to die. He told the mariners that he was running from the Lord and that his God caused the storm. However, Jonah received a class on the depth of God's mercy. God's mercy was as deep as the sea. And God prepared a storm for Jonah's stubbornness.

Does God bring spiritual storms? Yes He does! If we have ever been chastened by God, we know it's a good thing. God's storms are actually His mercy and the proof of His love for us. If we are without chastisement then we are illegitimate.

"But if ye be without chastisement, whereof all are partakers, then are ye bastards, and not sons." (Hebrews 12:8)

We understand how much God loves us not by how we deal with Him, but how He deals with us. Thank God for His chastening, because He loves us. We can't get away with anything because the Holy Spirit chastens and convicts us.

Satan brings spiritual storms also. However Satan's storms are not meant to chasten or discipline us, they are meant to destroy us. How do we know the difference between God's storms and Satan's? In essence, sin opens the door to receiving storms from God.

God brings storms for correction when we disobey His instructions. Nevertheless, God in His mercy is ready to forgive any sin we have committed. The only sin God cannot forgive is the sin we will not confess. Stubbornness and a hard heart prohibit us from admitting we are wrong and God is right. If we look long enough and hard enough, we'll find God's mercy in His chastening. So, let's learn to accept His storms and resist the devil's.

The devil brings storms of opposition and resistance to every move of God. Whenever God tells us to do something, here comes the devil with a storm to oppose God's will for our lives. If we are faint-hearted and quit, then we will never overcome the storms the devil brings against us. We must have the stuff that sticks and persistence helps us to overcome the opposition and resistance of the enemy.

However, we cannot use persistence if the storm is from God. If we do, we are operating in disobedience, rebellion and stubbornness.

Jonah used persistence and ended up in the belly of a fish for three days and three nights. Jonah disobeyed God; moved into a place of rebellion and stubbornness, which is as the sin of witchcraft (1st Sam. 15:23). When this occurs Satan can manipulate, intimidate, exploit, and dominate our lives.

The word chastening means *the father's correction; discipline and punishment.* The Father's love compels us through discipline, correction and sometimes punishment. The Bible says if a father does not use the rod of correction or discipline his son, he does not love him (Prov. 13:24). Love is a many splendored thing and we know our heavenly Father truly loves us. In His love we are not consumed, by His mercy we just receive chastening to align us back into His will.

—We Must Learn to Receive Mercy—

> *"They that observe lying vanities forsake their own mercy. But I will sacrifice unto thee with the voice of thanksgiving; I will pay that I have vowed. Salvation is of the LORD. And the LORD spake unto the fish, and it vomited out Jonah upon the dry land."* (Jonah 2:8-10)

After the chastening, Jonah was convicted and he repented. When we confess our sins, not only does God forgive us, He also cleanses us. We don't experience condemnation but reconciliation.

Some never receive God's mercy and reconciliation because they cover up their sin. These unfortunate people are stuck in condemnation, guilt, inferiority, etc. Their spirits are never lifted when the Word is being preached. Instead, they go to church out of obligation not to worship God. In essence, they have lost their first love. They think if they miss church others will know they have backslidden; so they just show up. All the while, God knows where they are, who they are, and how they got there.

Mercy is the proof of God's love. If we have a broken heart and ask God's forgiveness, He is merciful. He will forgive and cleanse us from faults, failures and infractions (1st Jhn. 1:19). The devil cannot condemn us when we are right with God. The moment we confess our sin, we instantly receive God's mercy. The telltale sign of our love for the Lord is when we are uncomfortable in our sin.

Jonah's conviction caused repentance. When it comes to God we have only two options in life; either we will be compliant or given to complaint. The difference between these two words is where the letter 'i' is located. Just as complaint and compliant is determined by where we place the "i," it matters where we place our eyes in every situation. The devil plagues us with condemnation when we place our eyes on ourselves. God placates us with conviction when our eyes are on Him.

For instances, the children of Israel cried to leave Egypt; three days after God opened the Red Sea they complained. They were unable to enter the promise land because of their murmuring, whining, crying, arguing, fussing, fighting, fretting, disobedience, rebellion, stubbornness and complaining. They would not comply and therefore God kept them in the wilderness for forty years; just like He kept Jonah in the belly of the fish for three days and three nights. Jonah said, "*When my soul fainted within me I remembered the LORD: and my prayer came in unto thee, into thine holy temple* (Jon. 2:7)."

How did Jonah get out of the belly of the fish? He accepted the mercies of God. Jonah realized if he brought truth, God would give mercy. Mercy is the proof of God's love. Love is a many splendored thing.

The prodigal son's account depicts the Father's mercy toward us. When the son came to himself he said, *"I will go to my father and confess I have sinned against heaven, against him, and I am not worthy to be called his son* (Lu. 15:18-19)."

As the son approached the father's house he was immediately greeted with the father's love. His father ran, kissed and embraced him. The son's life was a miserable mess, but the grace and mercy of the father called for the best—the best robe, the best ring and the best celebration repentance could bring. The Father is still extending mercy toward us, today.

Once we are able to receive the Father's mercy we are prepared to distribute His love to those around us. The Bible says: *"Blessed are the merciful; for they shall obtain mercy* (Matt. 5:7)." The proof of love is revealed through mercy. There is a thin line between love and hate and that thin line is mercy.

We are not perfect or right all of the time; but God is merciful to us. Consider the following quote:

> *"He made known his ways unto Moses, his acts unto the children of Israel. The LORD is merciful and gracious, slow to anger, and plenteous in mercy."* (Psalms 103:7-8)

God is slow to anger and plenteous in mercy. He doesn't give us mercy for one day and that's it; no, He is plenteous in mercy. His mercy does not run out. David said, *"Surely goodness and mercy shall follow me all the days of my life...* (Psa. 23:6)." We don't deserve it, but He is still merciful and gracious to us.

The foundation of grace is mercy. Grace is God giving us what we do not deserve. *"For by grace are ye saved through faith; and that not of yourselves: it is the gift of God: Not of works, lest any man should boast* (Eph. 2:8-9)." Before we get the grace of God we get the mercy of God. We can never stand before God and say, "I deserved or earned this." No, God gave it to us.

God's mercy is holding back what we do deserve. There are punishments that we should have gotten, but God said, "No, I'm merciful." However, what good is God's mercy if we do not approach Him to receive it?

> *"Let us therefore come boldly unto the throne of grace, that we may obtain mercy, and find grace to help in time of need."* (Hebrews 4:16)

We can come boldly to the throne of grace not judgment, wherein we obtain mercy and find grace to assist us with the issues we face. As we receive God's mercy, we can become a testimony of it.

—Become a Testimony— of God's Mercy

Jonah was a testimony and sign of God's mercy. When Jonah

came to Ninevah he didn't have to preach much because the mariners were already there. They had told the people they threw Jonah overboard, and a great fish swallowed him whole. The Ninevites heard the preaching of the mariners, but had not seen a sign yet. However, when they saw Jonah, they concluded that if God was merciful to him, God could be merciful to them. The scriptures tell us that starting with their king, the Ninevites repented and God showed His mercy by not destroying them (Jon. 3:6-10). God is not a God that is out for payback; He is a just God that extends His mercy to us.

Jonah was a sign and testimony for God. His account declares God's mercy. If it had not been for the mercy of God I would not be here today. I'm sure all of us can say the same. Love is a many splendored thing and His grace and mercy endures forever.

> *"Incline your ear, and come unto me: hear, and your soul shall live; and I will make an everlasting covenant with you,* ***even the sure mercies of David."*** (Isaiah 55:3 boldness added)

Another patriarch we can look to as a testimony of God's mercy is David. The aforementioned passage mentioned the sure mercies of David. What are the sure mercies of David? David wrote about it in Psalms 51.

It all began when David saw Bathsheba, Uriah's wife and had an affair with her. In the process of time Bathsheba became pregnant with David's child. Seeking to cover up his sin, David called Uriah from the battlefield and told him to go spend time with his wife. Uriah was so loyal he refused the pleasure of his wife because his fellow soldiers were in the middle of battle.

Truly devoted, Uriah would not return home, he slept at the king's door. Now convinced that his sin would be discovered, David called his captain and told him to take Uriah back to the battlefield and put him on the front line. Uriah was killed and afterwards David made Bathsheba his wife (2nd Sam. 11:1-27).

The account continues in 2nd Samuel 12 where Nathan, David's preacher, tells him a story about a rich man stealing a poor man's only lamb. David's judgment was that the rich man should die. Nathan said to David, "You are the man." David fell to his knees and wept to God for mercy. David had an adulterous affair, committed murder and tried to cover it up; but he cried out for mercy.

> *"Have mercy upon me, O God, according to thy loving kindness: according unto the multitude of thy tender mercies blot out my transgressions. Wash me throughly from mine iniquity, and cleanse me from my sin. For I acknowledge my transgressions: and my sin is ever before me. Against thee, thee only, have I sinned, and done this evil in thy sight: that thou mightest be justified when thou speakest, and be clear when thou judgest. Behold, I was shapen in iniquity; and in sin did my mother conceive me. Behold, thou desirest truth in the inward parts: and in the hidden part thou shalt make me to know wisdom. Purge me with hyssop, and I shall be clean: wash me, and I shall be whiter than snow."* (Psalms 51:1-7)

David knew how to cry out to God. He said I have sinned

against thee; he admitted his transgression against Uriah; and acknowledged his iniquity which was something bent, twisted, and wrong on the inside of him. Only God can make the crooked thing straight in us (Isa. 45:2). David's confessed chicanery was met with God's love and cleansing.

Through David's atrocities we are witnesses of God's mercies. In essence, David became a testimony for God. If God cleansed David and allowed him to remain king, he will be merciful to us. The only sin God cannot forgive is the sin we will not confess.

> *"Mercy and truth are met together; righteousness and peace have kissed each other."* (Psalms 85:10)

God is calling a meeting with us. He will bring mercy, but He needs us to come with truth. If we come any other way He cannot extend His mercy.

Love is a many splendored thing and the Father's love reaches to restore us when we fall. We are living testimonies of God's love and mercy. We are trophies of His grace and forgiveness. Now, let us become extensions of His heart, proving His love by dispensing mercy to others.

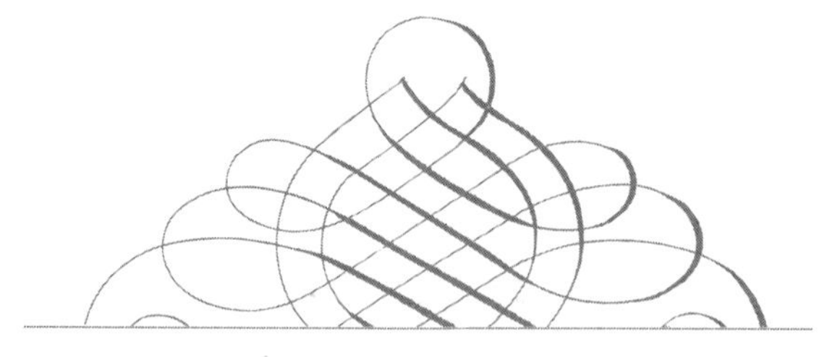

THE OBJECT OF OUR LOVE
JESUS

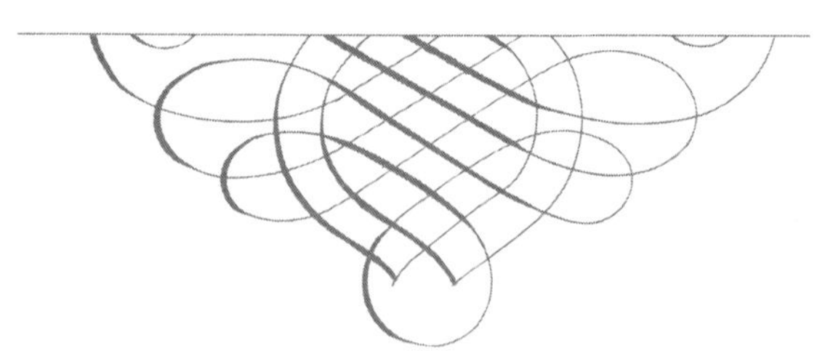

14

LOVING JESUS MORE THAN THESE

*"So when they had dined, Jesus saith to Simon Peter, Simon, son of Jonas, **lovest thou me more than these?** He saith unto him, Yea, Lord; thou knowest that I love thee. He saith unto him, Feed my lambs."*

(JOHN 21:15 BOLDNESS ADDED)

The context of the preceding passage provides us with the consummation of Jesus Christ's ministry (Acts 1:9). Prior to His ascension, Jesus had returned to His disciples to further instruct and train them concerning the vastness of God's love (Jhn. 21:15).

The greatest weapon against the adversary is love because love will never fail and love is the foundation for all manifestations and operations of God (1st Cor. 12:6).

As Christians, we must be baptized into the franchise of God's love, peace and blessing. It has been said, "You can't buy love." However, God's love does not come cheap. He paid for our sins through the giving of His Son (Jhn. 3:16). The ultimate symbol of Jesus' love for us is the cross.

There is never a question of God's love for us. There remains, however, a question of our love for Him. The inquiry is not with our affection for Jesus, but whether or not we desire Him more than everything else.

—LOVE JESUS MORE—

The Bible says God "*so loved*" and that "so" is a word that cannot be comprehended or articulated with our finite capacity of reasoning. Please understand it's not that God *just* loved us; we're not *just* one of God's loves; God *so* loved us. Love is a many splendored thing and to know that God "so" loves us should resonate in our hearts. It should resound throughout the rest of our lives causing us to love God in the same manner.

In John chapter 21, we find Jesus asking Peter, "*Do you love me more than these?*" And Peter says, "Yes, Lord!" Jesus responds to Peter and says, "*Feed my lambs.*" Jesus asks Peter a second time, "*Do you love me?*" and Peter said, "*Yea, Lord, you know that I love you.*" The response from the Lord is, "*Feed my sheep.*" Jesus then asks Peter a third and final time, "*Do you love me*?" Once again, Jesus says, "*Feed my sheep* (vs. 15-17)."

The love Jesus inquired of was agape, but the love Peter responded with was phileo. It is not enough to say we love God, we must settle the matter with undying and unconditional love. Nevertheless, we must not make Jesus one of the things we love in this world. We must give Him the preeminence in our lives.

We are to love God in such a distinct manner that it separates

Him from everyone and everything else. Our love for God is to be so exclusive that it puts Jesus at center stage and on a page all by Himself.

In John chapter 21, we find Peter decided to go fishing (vs. 3). In essence, Peter placed his affinity for fishing above his affection for Jesus' ministry.

> *"...If any man will come after me, let him deny himself, and take up his cross, and follow me. For whosoever will save his life shall lose it: and whosoever will lose his life for my sake shall find it."* (Matthew 16:24-25)

Vines translates the word "deny" as "*aparneomi*." It means to *forget and lose sight of one's self and one's own interests.*

Peter came to the conclusion it was better to return to the thing he loved before he met Jesus—fishing. Consequently, Peter failed to *deny* himself, even worse; he *lost* himself in his will and not God's.

Jesus said in the latter portion of John 5:30, "*I seek not mine own will, but the will of the Father which hath sent me.*" The real power is the will power. Peter's decision affected the other disciples because he was the leader of the group.

> *"Simon Peter said to them, I am going fishing! They said to him, And we are coming with you! So they went out and got into the boat, and throughout that night they caught nothing."* (John 21:3 AMP)

Peter's derailment caused others to get off track. When we cease loving and committing ourselves to serve the Lord's cause, we become ineffective. Throughout the night, Peter and the others did not catch a single fish!

> *"But when the morning was now come, Jesus stood on the shore: but the disciples knew not that it was Jesus. Then Jesus saith unto them, Children, have ye any meat? They answered him, No. And he said unto them, Cast the net on the right side of the ship, and ye shall find. They cast therefore, and now they were not able to draw it for the multitude of fishes. Therefore, that disciple whom Jesus loved saith unto Peter, It is the Lord. Now when Simon Peter heard that it was the Lord, he girt his fisher's coat unto him, (for he was naked,) and did cast himself into the sea."* (John 21:4-7)

When the disciples followed the instructions of Jesus, they did not have to toil. Jesus caused the fish to come to them. There were so many fish in the net; the disciples were unable to pull in the load.

When we place Jesus first in our lives, we'll experience success. Our success may not be without struggle, but with Jesus there's no need for stress. Peter's frustration developed once he took his eyes off Jesus and placed it on something else (fish).

In the midst of the disciple's toiling Jesus appears to ask a particular question—"Children, have you any meat (Jhn. 21:5)?" Jesus' inquiry of the disciples work is critical for all of us. In essence, Jesus was asking them, "Are the other objects of your affection working for you?" This question is timeless and certainly applies to us today.

> *"As soon then as they were come to land, they saw a fire of coals there, and fish laid thereon, and bread. Jesus saith unto them, Bring of the fish which ye have now caught. Simon Peter went up, and drew the net to land full of great fishes, an hundred and fifty and three: and for all there were so many, yet was not the net broken. Jesus saith unto them, Come and dine...."* (John 21:9-12)

After the disciples finished their meal with Jesus, He asked, *"Peter, do you love me more than these* (vs. 15)*?"* "*These*" means everything; we are not going to disqualify anything. In the case of the disciples it was going fishing, with us, "these" could be our family, finances, material possessions, etc. God is not opposed to us having things. However, God is opposed to things having us.

No matter if its people or things, we must establish that we love Jesus more. If we love people or things *more than* we love Him, they become our god. The very first commandment God established is, *"Thou shall have no other gods before me* (Ex. 20:3)*."* Love is a many splendored thing! Whatever we own, we have it because God loves us.

> *"The earth is the LORD'S, and the fullness thereof; the world, and they that dwell therein."* (Psalms 24:1)

Someone may ask, "What about my love for my husband, wife, children, or my parents?" We are to love our families. We are to love our spouse. Why marry them if we do not love them? The point is to make sure our love for them never exceeds our love for Jesus.

Jesus does not want to be a name on our love list. He desires to be the object of our love and not reduced to a list of our loves. Whatever we do, or whoever we love extends from our love for Him.

> *"And whatsoever ye do, do it* ***heartily, as to the Lord,*** *and not unto men. Knowing that of the Lord ye shall receive the reward of the inheritance: for ye serve the Lord Christ."* (Colossians 3:23-24 boldness added)

The etymology of the word heartily (*kardia*) carries the meaning of "*the hidden springs of the personal life*" or "*the sphere of Divine influence.*" Kardia also represents or contains "*the true character of a person.*"[47]

Loving heartily causes us to endure hardships and not quit. A divinely influenced person of true character loves their family, friends and everybody else because they love the Lord. When a person really loves someone or something they are willing to make a sacrifice.

If we love Jesus, there's always sacrifice involved. The Apostle Paul understood love with sacrifice:

> *"I have been crucified with Christ [in Him I have shared His crucifixion]; it is no longer I who live, but Christ (the Messiah) lives in me; and the life I now live in the body I live by faith in (by adherence to and reliance on and complete trust in) the Son of God, Who loved me and gave Himself up for me."* (Galatians 2:20 AMP)

At the core of Paul's willingness to sacrifice was the revelation of God's love for him personally. Vine's says that to "*be crucified with Christ*" metaphorically means a renunciation of the world that characterizes the authentic Christian life.

Paul wrote to the church at Galatia that he "*died with Christ.*" He renounced everything he possessed and became a follower of Christ.

To the church at Philippi, Paul wrote:

> *"Yea doubtless, and I count all things but loss for the excellency of the knowledge of Christ Jesus my Lord: for whom I have suffered the loss of all things, and do count them but dung, that I may win Christ."* (Philippians 3:8)

In his exhortation to the Philippian church, the Apostle Paul became a living lesson of loving Jesus more. Everything Paul accomplished educationally and religiously; he counted *as dung (excrement)* that he may win Christ. Paul heartily declared to the church, "I love Jesus more than these!"

There are many who say they love God but fail to serve Him. They are not willing to sacrifice their time, talents, gifts, possessions or their money. This indicates their lack of love for Jesus.

—Loving Jesus More— Than the World

Believe it or not, God loves us no less than He loves Jesus. This profound revelation should cause us to keep ourselves in the Father's love. Keeping ourselves in the center of the love of God protects us from being engrossed by the perverseness of the world.

This world offers the fulfillment of desires apart from God's will. Jesus wants us to have our desires as long as they are connected to the Father's will for our lives.

> *"Therefore I say unto you, What things soever ye desire, when ye pray, believe that ye receive them, and ye shall have them."* (Mark 11:24)

> *"Delight thyself also in the Lord: and he shall give thee the desires of thine heart."* (Psalms 37:4)

God *so* loved Adam and Eve that He placed gold and precious gems in Eden for them to enjoy.

> *"And a river went out of Eden to water the garden; and from thence it was parted, and became into four heads. The name of the first is Pison: that is it which compasseth the whole land of Havilah,* ***where there is gold; And the gold of that land is good:*** *there is bdellium and the* ***onyx stone.****"*
> (Genesis 2:10-12 boldness added)

Beloved, God is not telling us that we cannot enjoy things that are in this world. He put the gold and the precious stones in Eden for Adam and Eve! However, once they placed their desires for things above their desire to please Him, they were forced to leave Eden with all of its wealth (Gen. 3:23-24).

Jesus says: "*But seek ye first the kingdom of God, and his righteousness; and all these things shall be added unto you* (Matt. 6:33)." God says, I want to add these things, just *do not seek the things*!

As we seek God *first*, we say to Him, "I love Jesus more than any and everything else!" Vine's says the word seek carries the meaning of "*desire, coveting earnestly, striving after, to obtain the things that are above.*"

The Bible admonishes:

> *"Love not the world, neither the things that are in the world. If any man love the world, the love of the Father is not in him. For all that is in the world, the lust of the flesh, and the lust of the eyes, and the pride of life, is not of the Father, but is of the world."* (1st John 2:15-16)

The "*lust of the flesh*" connotes having an intense *passion*. To fully appreciate the term flesh we must remove the letter "h" off the word *flesh* and spell it backwards. When we do this we see the word *self.* Hence, the lust of the flesh is a selfish passion and pursuit for things and people not for Jesus.

The American Heritage Dictionary says that passion carries the meaning of a "*powerful compelling emotion or desire.*" Passion is a strong motivator. Jesus had a passion for us. We know it as, "The passion of Christ." His passion for us took Him to the cross. Our passion for Him should cause us to carry our cross with a passion for what He wants.

Without a passion for Jesus, we are left with a passion or lust for the things the flesh desires. Here's a gruesome reality, the flesh has a way of having a passion for flesh. It does not matter what sex the flesh is just as long as it's flesh. One of the ways flesh is described in the original Greek is (*sarx*) *"the seat of sin in man."*[48] The lust of the flesh is the *passion* of the sinful nature that is seated in man.

The *"lust of the eyes"* is the desire for *possessions*. The mindset is I love everything I see. Many squandered thousands and some millions of dollars because of the pursuit of possessions! For these people enough is never enough. Instead of loving and pursuing Jesus more, they pursue more and more possessions!

Then there is the *"pride of life."* This is an ardent desire for *positions* in this world. For many the love of a position withholds them from loving God.

Those inflicted with the pride of life are not infatuated with work, just the title or position it holds. They seek the position for the prestige, and prominence attached to it.

> "*The world passeth away, and the lust thereof: but he that doeth the will of God abideth forever.*" (1st John 2:17)

Love is a many splendored thing. God's love places us first and our love should give Him priority over everything. We must establish nothing competes with Jesus. If we love Jesus more, that conviction keeps us from compromising.

A conviction is a "*fixed or firm belief.*" The principle of our conviction should be based upon who Jesus is. Unfortunately, many do not have any convictions at all. Therefore, they are willing to compromise everything and anything. However, our conviction for Jesus should cause us to make major impacts in the lives of others.

Jesus said:

> *"Sanctify them through thy truth: thy word is truth. As thou hast sent me into the world, even so have I also sent them into the world."* (John 17:17-18)

Jesus prayed His disciples would be "*sanctified through truth.*" He wanted them to make an impact upon the world. Jesus did not want them to be *isolated*, rather *insulated* to ensure they would never be *contaminated* by the world.

> *"And he ordained twelve, that they should be with him, and that he might send them forth to preach,* ***And to have power*** *to heal sicknesses, and to cast out devils."*
> (Mark 3:14-15 boldness added)

Ordained is the Greek word "*poyeho.*"[49] Which means to "*make ready, to lead one out, to prepare to put one forth.*" These twelve disciples were ordained, prepared and given power. Therefore, Jesus declared as the Father sent Him into the world, He sends us. As disciples of Jesus, we are insulated and sanctified through the truth (Jhn. 17:17).

This truth by which we have been sanctified is seen in Jesus' love for us. Jesus ordains those He loves to be with Him. His Word is truth and we must love His Word.

—Loving Jesus' Word More—

> *"If ye keep my commandments, ye shall abide in my love; even as I have kept my Father's commandments, and abide in his love."* (John 15:10)

There is a combination that unlocks the treasures of the Father's will for our lives. This combination is abiding and obeying. It is not enough to abide in Jesus' salvation; we need His Word abiding in us. *"If ye abide in me, and my words abide in you, ye shall ask what ye will, and it shall be done unto you* (Jhn. 15:7)." We must abide in the Father's love and obey the Father's Word which conveys His heart.

There is a tributary of our church we refer to as *S.W.A.T. (Soul Winning Action Team)*. The SWAT team operates monthly in the spirit of the following scripture:

> *"And the lord said unto the servant, Go out into the highways and hedges, and compel them to come in, that my house may be filled."* (Luke 14:23)

The SWAT team enters different communities in the surrounding cities, going door to door, sharing the love of God through the Word of God. One particular outing, a person answered his door with a gun, but after hearing the gospel and the love of God, he gave his life to Jesus! In another section of town, a SWAT member was confronted by a pit bull! Yet, the love of God radiated from the SWAT member; and it caused the pit bull to back up and cower down. Glory to God!

Jesus emphatically stated:

> *"Behold, I give unto you power to tread on serpents and scorpions, and over all the power of the enemy: and nothing shall by any means hurt you."* (Luke 10:19)

Above all, God's power is found in His Word and His Word impacts all with His love. The world wants to hear about His love. He is our hope. God's love is packaged in His Word and His Word is a living organism. The word is alive; it encourages and instructs us. Jesus declared His words are spirit and life (Jhn. 6:63).

The Word of God gives us power to stand, no matter what happens (Eph. 6:13). When we receive the word of God by His love, something happens on the inside. The Spirit of God's love begins to *stir up the gift* inside us. That gift is God's love (2nd Tim. 1:6-7).

When the word is preached, the Holy Spirit begins to move. If all we have is the Word and no Spirit, we *dry up*. If all we have is the Spirit and no Word, we *blow up*. It takes the word and the Spirit to *stir us up.*

Nehemiah made an impact on people with God's Word. He encouraged his leaders and all who possessed the Word of God to distribute it to those who were without it. The results cause great jubilation.

> *"So they read in the book in the law of God distinctly, and gave the sense, and caused them to understand the reading... And all the people went their way to eat, and to drink, and to send portions, and to make great mirth, because they had understood the words that were declared unto them."* (Nehemiah 8:8,12)

We must celebrate having the Word of God. When we love Jesus we come to love and appreciate His Word. His Word brings light where there is darkness; life where there is death; and love where there is a dearth of it. *"In the beginning was the Word, and the Word was with God, and the Word was God* (Jhn. 1:1)."

> *"All scripture is given by inspiration of God, and is profitable for doctrine, for reproof, for correction, for instruction in righteousness."* (2nd Timothy 3:16)

When we have a love for Jesus' Word there's a love for His instructions. Some cannot stand instructions. Now, they seek direction in life, so they ask for correction. However, they fail to understand that instruction is the prerequisite for correction. There is no sense in correcting if there is no instruction. Therefore, to love Jesus more means to love His instructions, correction and direction for our lives.

Jesus is always about correcting us. His Word makes the crooked things straight (Isa. 42:16). God's love brings correction not criticism. Correction without instruction is criticism. Some people are quick to criticize others without instructions.

That is what the world does, but Jesus gives us instruction and correction in righteousness. They go hand in hand. We cannot have one without the other.

In conveying a tragic mindset, Solomon exposed:

> *"...How have I* ***hated instruction****, and my heart despised reproof; And have not* ***obeyed the voice of my teachers****, nor* ***inclined mine ear to them that instructed me!*** *I was almost in all evil in the midst of the congregation and assembly."* (Proverbs 5:12-14 boldness added)

The Theological Wordbook of the Old Testament the word hate (*"sane"*) carries the meaning of to "*be set against.*" It also states that "*sane*" expresses an "*emotional attitude toward persons and things which are opposed, detested, despised and with which one wishes to have no contact or relationship. It is therefore* ***the opposite of love****. Whereas love draws and unites, hate separates and keeps distant.*"

Solomon addresses the tragedy of a person that refuses and despises instruction and therefore cannot be corrected. We must keep a sincere love for God's Word in our hearts and receive the Lord's instruction with joy. If Jesus cannot instruct us, He cannot correct us into living the best life.

Love is a many splendored thing. Because of love, Jesus took the time to instruct and correct Peter concerning his love life (Jhn. 21). The same question Jesus asked Peter then, He asks us now, "Do you love me *MORE* than these?" The answer for me, as I know it is for you is, "Yes Lord! I love you *MORE* than these!"

> *"For I am persuaded, that neither death, nor life, nor angels, nor principalities, nor powers, nor things present, nor things to come, Nor height, nor depth, nor any other creature, shall be able to separate us from the love of God, which is in Christ our Lord."* (Romans 8:38-39)

ALL IN THE NAME OF LOVE

The following recap highlights several excerpts from "Love a Many Splendored Thing." In the Sermon on the Mount we find our Lord teaching three very important concepts:

1) The example of God's Love
2) The extent of God's Love
3) The excitement about God's Love

—The Example of God's Love—

Let's begin our exploration with the example of God's love.

The example of God's love is found in John 3:16: "For God so loved the world, that he gave his only begotten Son..." The emphasis on "so loved" is a many splendored thing. It is all-inclusive, as it applies to the entire world. Everyone is loved by God.

May I hasten to say that no one's birth was by accident, neither incident nor coincident; it was Provident. No one came into the world without God's permission. This is not to say or blame God for causing deplorable and heinous actions such as rape or incest that might have ultimately resulted in a birth. The Lord will never cause anyone to commit sin. No, that's Satan's modus operandi.

However, when the example of God's love is at work, God can take the bitter, make it better, and bring forth the BEST! Only God can make the crooked straight (Isaiah 45:2).

The following scripture teaches one of the divine principles in life:

> *"But when the fulness of the time was come, God sent forth his Son, made of a woman, made under the law, To redeem them that were under the law..."* (Galatians 4:4-5)

This divine principle correlates with the example of God's love because when the world was in need of the Savior, God sent forth His son to redeem mankind.

According to this divine principle these are essential:

1) The Right Period—The fullness of time; we were born at the right time.

2) The Right Person—God sent forth His Son; He has also sent us forth. We are the right people at the right time.

3) The Right Purpose—Jesus was born to redeem mankind; we were born with a purpose in mind.

The example of God's love allowed us to come in the right period. We're the right people. We're here for the right purpose. The foundation of the revelation of our purpose is love. Love is a many splendored thing.

—The Extent of God's Love—

The extent of God's love is to love everybody. I know we may ask, "How can I love people I don't even know?" Simple, if we don't know them, we have no true reason to hate them.

The extent of God's love is given in the following passage:

> *"That ye may be the children of your Father which is in heaven: for he maketh his sun to rise on the evil and on the good, and sendeth rain on the just and on the unjust."* (Matthew 5:45)

That is the extent of the breadth of God's love. He loves everyone, unconditionally. It is called agape.

The depth of His love is that He didn't give animals, silver, or gold, He gave His only begotten Son. He loves us so deeply that He bankrupted heaven to buy us back. There was no way to save us without the shedding of the Son's innocent blood.

> *"This is my commandment, That ye love one another, as I have loved you. Greater love hath no man than this, that a man lay down his life for his friends."* (John 15:12-13)

Jesus commands us to love like God loves, with agape love, unconditionally. In contrast the world's love is shown in the following text:

"For if ye love them which love you, what reward have ye? do not even the publicans the same? And if ye salute your brethren only, what do ye more than others? do not even the publicans so?" (Matthew 5:46-47)

The extent of the world's love is narrow and shallow. They love only those who love, greet, and give to them. However, we are admonished to: *"Be ye therefore perfect even as your father which is in Heaven is perfect* (Matthew 5:48)."

—THE EXCITEMENT— ABOUT GOD'S LOVE

The excitement about God's love is that it can become our own. The excitement is in knowing we can love like God. 1st John 4:17 tells us, *"...because as he is, so are we in this world."* Our excitement comes when we emulate our heavenly Father and *"so love the world* (Jhn. 3:16)." There is a revelation of a difference in the love of John 3:16 and 1st John 2:15. The first refers to loving people, the other to loving the world's system. The excitement of God's love is a many splendored thing!

There are three types of people that can't and won't function in the excitement of loving like God. First, *unsaved* people will not function in God's love. One must be born from above, in order to love like God loves. Second, *unforgiving* people will not function in God's love. Most worldly people and people of the world carry un-forgiveness. Third, *unaware* people will not function in God's love. Those unaware of the Father's love can't love like Him.

As saints we can love people we don't like. Loving and liking are two separate things. Don't confuse loving someone with liking someone.

Remember, the key to the excitement of God's love becoming our love is found in practicing perfected love (Matthew. 5:48 and 1st John 4:11-12). *"If you do something against someone that you dislike, you dislike the person more, but if you do something good to someone you dislike, you will dislike them less and even begin to like them!"*

In pursuit of love we must "Learn to Do Well (Isaiah 1:17)!" In Matthew 5:44 Jesus taught:

1) Bless them
2) Do good to them
3) Pray for them

Jesus shared the greatest commandment called "The Shema of Israel:"

> *"And Jesus answered him, The first of all the commandments is, Hear, O Israel; The Lord our God is one Lord: And thou shalt love the Lord thy God with all thy heart, and with all thy soul, and with all thy mind, and with all thy strength: this is the first commandment. And the second is like, namely this, Thou shalt love thy neighbour as thyself. There is none other commandment greater than these."* (Mark 12:29-31)

It must be understood, when we love God vertically it will manifest horizontally. Consider this: the first letter in the word love is "L." The letter "L" extends both vertically (to God) and horizontally (to others).

That's what the parable of The Good Samaritan is all about.

> *"But a certain Samaritan, as he journeyed, came where he was: and when he saw him, he had compassion on him."* (Luke 10:33)

Jesus taught love in action is compassion. To love God with all our heart, soul, mind and strength is to reach out with compassion and love to others. This is accomplished by *staying in the love of God and stopping in the name of love.*

It is exciting to know we can love like God. Some may ask, "What's love got to do with it?" Love has everything to do with it. Love never fails because love is a many splendored thing.

ENDNOTES

INTRODUCTION

1. Harper, Douglas, Compiler. Online Etymological Dictionary [Internet]. Copyright 2000 [Cited September 3, 2013]. Available from: http://www.etymonline.com/.

2. Harper, Douglas, Compiler. Online Etymological Dictionary [Internet]. Copyright 2000 [Cited September 3, 2013]. Available from: http://www.etymonline.com/.

3. Vines, William Edwy. Vines Expository Dictionary of Old and New Testament Words [Internet]. Copyright 1940 [Cited September 3, 2013]. Available from: http://studybible.info/vines/.

4. Vines, William Edwy. Vines Expository Dictionary of Old and New Testament Words [Internet]. Copyright 1940 [Cited September 3, 2013]. Available from: http://studybible.info/vines/.

5. Successories Online [Internet]. Copyright 1985. [Cited September 3, 2013]. Available from: http://www.successories.com.

CHAPTER 1

6. Wales, Jimmy, Sanger, Larry, Stallman, Richard, Founders. Wikipedia [Internet]. Copyright March 16, 2001. Article Philadelphia [Internet] [Cited September 3, 2013]. Available from: http://www.wikipedia.org/wiki/Philadelphia.

7. Vines, William Edwy. Vines Expository Dictionary of Old and New Testament Words [Internet]. Copyright 1940 [Cited September 3, 2013]. Available from: http://studybible.info/vines/.

8. Leadership Ministries Worldwide, Author. Preachers Outline and Sermon Commentary [Bible Software]. Commentary on Genesis 6, Genesis 29 and John 11. Copyright September 1, 2003.

9. Zavada, Jack, What Is Eros? About Christianity. [Internet] Copyright 1996. [Cited September 3, 2013]. Available from: http://www. christianity.about.com/od/glossary/a/Eros.htm.

10. Carr, G. Lloyd. Tyndale Old Testament Commentary, The Song of Solomon. [Cited September 3, 2013] Intervarsity Press, 2009, pg.76.

CHAPTER 2

11. Vines, William Edwy. Vines Expository Dictionary of Old and New Testament Words [Internet]. Copyright 1940 [Cited September 5, 2013]. Available from: http://studybible.info/vines/.

12. Vines, William Edwy. Vines Expository Dictionary of Old and New Testament Words [Internet]. Copyright 1940 [Cited September 5, 2013]. Available from: http://studybible.info/vines/.

13. Vines, William Edwy. Vines Expository Dictionary of Old and New Testament Words [Internet]. Copyright 1940 [Cited September 5, 2013]. Available from: http://studybible.info/vines/.

14. Stein, Jess, Editor. Random House Dictionary. [Internet]. Copyright 1966 [Cited September 27, 2013]. Available from: http://www.dictionary.com

15. Vines, William Edwy. Vines Expository Dictionary of Old and New Testament Words [Internet]. Copyright 1940 [Cited September 5, 2013]. Available from: http://studybible.info/vines/.

CHAPTER 4

16. Vines, William Edwy. Vines Expository Dictionary of Old and New Testament Words [Internet]. Copyright 1940 [Cited September 6, 2013]. Available from: http://studybible.info/vines/.

17. Nelson Mandela Foundation [Internet]. Copyright 2013 Nelson Mandela Centre of Memory. [Cited December 12, 2013]. Available from: http://www.nelsonmandela.org/content/page/biography.

CHAPTER 5

18. Vines, William Edwy. Vines Expository Dictionary of Old and New Testament Words [Internet]. Copyright 1940 [Cited September 10, 2013]. Available from: http://studybible.info/vines/.

CHAPTER 6

19. Vines, William Edwy. Vines Expository Dictionary of Old and New Testament Words [Internet]. Copyright 1940 [Cited September 12, 2013]. Available from: http://studybible.info/vines/.

20. Vines, William Edwy. Vines Expository Dictionary of Old and New Testament Words [Internet]. Copyright 1940 [Cited September 5, 2013]. Available from: http://studybible.info/vines/.

21. Vines, William Edwy. Vines Expository Dictionary of Old and New Testament Words [Internet]. Copyright 1940 [Cited September 5, 2013]. Available from: http://studybible.info/vines/.

CHAPTER 7

22. Vines, William Edwy. Vines Expository Dictionary of Old and New Testament Words [Internet]. Copyright 1940 [Cited September 14, 2013]. Available from: http://studybible.info/vines/.

23. Vines, William Edwy. Vines Expository Dictionary of Old and New Testament Words [Internet]. Copyright 1940 [Cited September 5, 2013]. Available from: http://studybible.info/vines/.

24. Vines, William Edwy. Vines Expository Dictionary of Old and New Testament Words [Internet]. Copyright 1940 [Cited September 5, 2013]. Available from: http://studybible.info/vines/.

25. Vines, William Edwy. Vines Expository Dictionary of Old and New Testament Words [Internet]. Copyright 1940 [Cited September 5, 2013]. Available from: http://studybible.info/vines/.

26. Vines, William Edwy. Vines Expository Dictionary of Old and New Testament Words [Internet]. Copyright 1940 [Cited September 5, 2013]. Available from: http://studybible.info/vines/.

CHAPTER 8

27. Vines, William Edwy. Vines Expository Dictionary of Old and New Testament Words [Internet]. Copyright 1940 [Cited September 16, 2013]. Available from: http://studybible.info/vines/.

28. Vines, William Edwy. Vines Expository Dictionary of Old and New Testament Words [Internet]. Copyright 1940 [Cited September 5, 2013]. Available from: http://studybible.info/vines/.

CHAPTER 9

29. Vines, William Edwy. Vines Expository Dictionary of Old and New Testament Words [Internet]. Copyright 1940 [Cited September 20, 2013]. Available from: http://studybible.info/vines/.

30. Wayne Goodman, The First Epistle General of Peter, The Tyndale New Testament Commentaries, Intervarsity Press, August 2009, pg. 168.

31. Vines, William Edwy. Vines Expository Dictionary of Old and New

Testament Words [Internet]. Copyright 1940 [Cited September 20, 2013]. Available from: http://studybible.info/vines/.

32. Vines, William Edwy. Vines Expository Dictionary of Old and New Testament Words [Internet]. Copyright 1940 [Cited September 20, 2013]. Available from: http://studybible.info/vines/.

33. Vines, William Edwy. Vines Expository Dictionary of Old and New Testament Words [Internet]. Copyright 1940 [Cited September 20, 2013]. Available from: http://studybible.info/vines/.

34. Vines, William Edwy. Vines Expository Dictionary of Old and New Testament Words [Internet]. Copyright 1940 [Cited September 20, 2013]. Available from: http://studybible.info/vines/.

CHAPTER 10

35. Vines, William Edwy. Vines Expository Dictionary of Old and New Testament Words [Internet]. Copyright 1940 [Cited September 27, 2013]. Available from: http://studybible.info/vines/.

36. Vines, William Edwy. Vines Expository Dictionary of Old and New Testament Words [Internet]. Copyright 1940 [Cited September 27, 2013]. Available from: http://studybible.info/vines/.

37. Stein, Jess, Editor. Random House Dictionary. [Internet]. Copyright 1966 [Cited September 27, 2013]. Available from: http://www.dictionary.com

38. Wales, Jimmy, Sanger, Larry, Stallman, Richard, Founders. Wikipedia [Internet]. Copyright March 16, 2001. Article Philadelphia [Internet] [Cited November 4, 2013]. Available from: http://en.wikipedia.org/wiki/Pledge_of_allegiance

39. Harper, Douglas, Compiler. Online Etymological Dictionary [Internet]. Copyright 2000 [Cited September 3, 2013]. Available from: http://www.etymonline.com/.

40. Vines, William Edwy. Vines Expository Dictionary of Old and New Testament Words [Internet]. Copyright 1940 [Cited September 27, 2013]. Available from: http://studybible.info/vines/.

CHAPTER 11

41. Vines, William Edwy. Vines Expository Dictionary of Old and New Testament Words [Internet]. Copyright 1940 [Cited November 4, 2013]. Available from: http://studybible.info/vines/.

42. Vines, William Edwy. Vines Expository Dictionary of Old and New Testament Words [Internet]. Copyright 1940 [Cited September 27, 2013]. Available from: http://studybible.info/vines/.

CHAPTER 12

43. Vines, William Edwy. Vines Expository Dictionary of Old and New Testament Words [Internet]. Copyright 1940 [Cited September 27, 2013]. Available from: http://studybible.info/vines/.

44. Vines, William Edwy. Vines Expository Dictionary of Old and New Testament Words [Internet]. Copyright 1940 [Cited September 27, 2013]. Available from: http://studybible.info/vines/.

45. Vines, William Edwy. Vines Expository Dictionary of Old and New Testament Words [Internet]. Copyright 1940 [Cited November 6, 2013]. Available from: http://studybible.info/vines/.

46. Harper, Douglas, Compiler. Online Etymological Dictionary [Internet]. "Habit." Copyright 2000 [Cited November 6, 2013]. Available from: http://www.etymonline.com/.

CHAPTER 14

47. Harris, R. Laird, Gleason L. Archer, Bruce K. Waltke, ed. Theological Wordbook of the Old Testament. "Sane." Accessed November 8, 2013. WORDsearch CROSS e-book. Chicago: Moody Press, 1980.

48. Practical Word Studies in The New Testament. Chattanooga: Leadership Ministries Worldwide, 1998. WORDsearch CROSS e-book.

49. Vines, William Edwy. Vines Expository Dictionary of Old and New Testament Words [Internet]. Copyright 1940 [Cited November 8, 2013]. Available from: http://studybible.info/vines/.

Charles Jenkins - Just to Know Him

My Redeemer sent to a rugged cross to set me free, My Saviour beared my sins just to Rescue me, My Replacement took my place so I wouldn't have to die, My Provider Now I have everlasting life.

2x

Just to Know Him 2x
Jesus Christ the Son of the Living God

Just to Know Him 2x
Jesus Christ the Son of the Living God.

Risen Savior Rose from the dead So I could rise again, Awesome Ruler Crucified just to call me friend. Hope of Glory One day I will get to see His face. I am grateful He Cared me enough to gladly take my place

~~Just~~ to Know Him 2x
~~Jesus Christ~~
Oh how He cares for you for me. ~~4x~~